DIAGNOSTIC FEATURES

DIAGNOSTIC FEATURES
NICK VIVEIROS

Absolutely no artificial intelligence (AI) was used in the writing of the contents of this book. The author just loves em dashes.

ISBN: 979-8-218-46036-5

DIAGNOSTIC FEATURES

NICK VIVEIROS

For my people –
thank you, thank you, thank you.

Table of Contents

Preface   1

1. Frantic efforts to avoid real or imagined abandonment.

Introduction to Criterion One   15
Space for Us   19
Birthday   20
Mammogram   21
Attachment   22
Isolation   23
The Houseparty   24
Midwinter   25
Third Phase   26
Scabs   27
Five O'Clock   28
California & Montgomery   29
Intuitions   30
Book of Worries   31
Meditation on *La Gitana*   32
Detachment   33

2. A pattern of unstable and intense interpersonal relationships characterized by alternating between extremes of idealization and devaluation.

Introduction to Criterion Two   35
About Autumn   39
Yearn   40
O Woman   41
Indictment   42
Lovebirds   43
************, Sunset, October   44
Epiphany   45
If & When   46
Vignette View of You & William Blake   47
May   48

New Year's   49
Letter to Sarah   50
Plymouth, July 6th, 4:45 AM   51
Transatlantic Red-Eye, Boston to London   52
Curlew   53
At the Metropolitan Ballet   54
Durham   55

3. Identity disturbance: markedly and persistently unstable self-image or sense of self.

Introduction to Criterion Three   57
Buffalo, New York   61
David Rakoff, Canada, August 17th, 2012   62
Everyone   63
Inside   64
Eighth Avenue Local, Sunday Morning   65
Some Days   66
Introductory Questions   67
Dead Winter   68
St. Valentine's Day   69
Man at 9th & Irving   70
Diagnostic Features   71
Equinox   72
Perfect Because   73

4. Impulsivity in at least two areas that are potentially self-damaging (e.g., spending, sex, substance abuse, reckless driving, binge eating).

Introduction to Criterion Four   75
Trains   79
Afternooning   80
Bad Habits   81
American Haiku / Impulses   82
American Haiku / Buying Cigarettes   82
American Haiku / Digits   82
American Haiku / Sober   82

DeKalb Avenue   83
Williamsburg   84
Closet Canticle   85
Plum Tree   86
6th & Minetta   87
Greyhound, Boston to Newport, Saturday Night   89
Blood Orange   90
Maverick & Chelsea   91
Benzodiazepines   92
Brother   93
203 Franklin Street   94
North Beach, Sunday Morning   95

5. Recurrent suicidal behavior, gestures, or threats, or self-mutilating behavior.

Introduction to Criterion Five   97
Haze   101
Burning   102
August 17th   103
The Omni Parker House   104
Staring from Sodom to Aquarius   105
Contrition   106
Contemplating   107
The Night   108
Gallows Hunting, East Boston   109
Belmont '19   110
Manchester Holiday Inn Express   111
Man on the Uptown 1 Train   112
Death Wish   113
Oceans Away   114

6. Affective instability due to a marked reactivity of mood (e.g., intense episodic dysphoria, irritability, or anxiety usually lasting a few hours and only rarely more than a few days).

Introduction to Criterion Six   115

102nd Floor, Empire State Building 119
June 120
Stinkboats 121
Autumn '16 122
November Blues 123
Chelsea Nights 124
Crossing Brooklyn Bridge 125
Walk Home Between Torrents 126
If 127
Machine 128
Somehow 129
Communication by Impact 130
March 21st 131

7. Chronic feelings of emptiness.

Introduction to Criterion Seven 133
The Patina Method 137
Dinner & A Film 138
Hoboken, New Jersey 139
Lamentation 140
Manna 141
Sundown 142
Flight 831, Boston to LaGuardia 143
Transmutations 144
Poem for Harlem 145
April, Counting the Dead 146
Church Street 147
Fireside 148
West Boylston, Massachusetts 149
Monday Morning 150

8. Inappropriate, intense anger or difficulty controlling anger.

Introduction to Criterion Eight 151
Holy ****! 155

Bastard   156
Personality   157
Borderline   158
Anniversaries   159
Hymn   160
Machiavelli   161
Weeding in the Late Afternoon   162
Akeldama   163

9. Transient, stress-related paranoid ideation or severe dissociative symptoms.

Introduction to Criterion Nine   165
Bengal Tiger   169
The Existentialist's Bible   170
Sylvia   171
Howl '17   172
Walking Campus   179
Illness   180
Antiphon   181
Daydreaming Up Impossible Situations   182
Hay Gente Aun Que Te Aman   183
Cause Proximate   184

Afterword and Acknowledgements   185

Resources   195

Preface

IT'S EARLY, SOMETIME BEFORE THE SUN comes up, and I'm sitting at an oversized oak table by the window of a dated hotel room at a golf resort, sifting through a very large stack of poetry covered in the little markings that have come to define my editing process as the late-summer sun rises over a row of southern pine.

I'd written a very boring and clinical preface for this collection before the manuscript was complete, which is very funny in that it perfectly epitomizes the approach I've taken to writing over the years: do now, think later. As I've done with many other aspects of my life these past few years, I tore it apart and rebuilt it honestly. I've been putting it off, and figured that there's no time quite like the present, sleepless in a hotel room hundreds of miles from home.

Life is very strange. I think of this as I look out the window onto the front of this hotel, where the sun is beginning to blue the sky from behind Duke University, shattering a solid wall of fir trees into a stained glass-looking thing. I sit at the table pulling on the end of a nicotine vape – my last vice, really – reading many of the poems you will read in this collection. Many of them stand in stark contrast to the

1

setting: a business meeting, at which I'm expected to be a business-like individual, free of any sort of neuroses that would prevent me from doing what I'm here to do.

I began writing poetry in sixth grade. We were asked to write about an experience we wanted to remember; I wrote a page and a half of verse about a recent trip to Boston with my family. It was good enough to earn me an A, which was the emotional equivalent of ecstasy to a child who was always trying to prove his worth. I kept writing, first as a means of doing something worth celebrating, and then out of a genuine love for the game. I wrote poems almost constantly, about anything and everything. It became an addiction. This collection contains around 10% of my total poetic output – 867 poems as of press time.

I loved to read as a child and teenager, and was lucky enough to find good heroes early. I wrote my high school thesis on James Baldwin. Jack Kerouac, Sylvia Plath, e.e. cummings, Mary Oliver, and Robert Lowell were early influences. For a while, I tried way too hard to be them (see Criterion 3). Once I stopped trying to be anyone but me, the quality of my work improved. You can see the influences of those poets in this collection, which includes some self-aware mimicry and some flattery.

At the end of a devastating year, I sat down to review my work. I was setting out on what turned into almost two years of intensive self-reflection and self-improvement. As I edited my work, it struck me that my collection resembled less of a cohesive narrative of my life than an amalgamation of different emotional experiences. I was always concerned that my poetry was emotionally dishonest – that I was writing to convince someone else of something – and for a while that was sort of true. I wanted to avoid the same mistakes I made in previous collections. As I did all those years ago, I wanted to write something worth celebrating,

2

but this time I wanted it to be entirely real, truly raw, and celebrated most by me.

I long believed that my poetry was so fragmented in nature, so sporadic and fitful in its composition, that it couldn't be compiled neatly into a collection with a clear message. Sorting through my hundreds of poems, it dawned on me that the best way to show the thing I'd wanted to show to people for years was to simply show it. As it turns out, my subconscious had done that work for me long ago.

Poetry is an intense medium, and borderline personality disorder is an intense illness, which makes them a good pair. A hallmark trait of borderline, diagnostic criterion six ("Affective instability due to a marked reactivity of mood"), is episodic emotional dysregulation. The borderline mind is overrun by intense emotions at startling speeds. I feel them all deeply, and have unconsciously documented that depth in my work. There are days on which I've experienced the intensity of the full spectrum of human emotion all at once, at full volume. I've written my way through all of them.

None of my attempts at self-understanding have ever seemed to capture the nature of my condition and my quirks quite like my poetry does. I write to process my emotions. As I sorted through those many poems, it became very clear to me that I could do two things at once: share these works with the world, and tell a story I've been searching for the words to tell for almost a decade.

It felt like a revelation from the divine. I couldn't believe I hadn't recognized it sooner. There was no other continuous thread through my body of work. I've written short poems and long screeds, loving observations and diatribes. They all wear different forms, strike different tones, and to an extent were written in different styles, but they all tell the same story: that of the intensity of my inner world.

With this in mind, I got to work digging through my poetic history, sorting each of the poems that I felt most strongly expressed the nine diagnostic criteria for borderline personality disorder into nine subcategories. It isn't a perfect system. Given the nature of borderline and its outsized impact on interpersonal relationships, there are many "love poems" outside of criterion 2 ("A pattern of unstable and intense interpersonal relationships"). There are poems that outline my unhealthy relationship with substances outside of criterion 4 ("Impulsivity in at least two areas that are potentially self-damaging").

The rule remains constant: if a poem most accurately portrays one of the nine criteria, or was written when I was experiencing that symptom of the condition in real-time, it's filed under that criterion. The poems in each section are all listed in (rough) chronological order. Through this lens, *Diagnostic Features* is three things: a dissection of the complex thing that I struggle with, a collection of my life's artistic work, and a personal history of that work and how it's changed over time.

I operated as an obsessive editor. Determined not to over-share for the sake of narrative at the expense of quality, I revised each poem, building them out and cutting them down again. A week after I began, I had a manuscript ready to print. At the time, I was lost in my condition. I knew I needed to be able to see things more clearly to publish a work I felt was worth publishing. Instead of pulling the trigger, I did a different thing and let it sit for a year and a half. There was no rush; to rush it would have defeated the purpose. To rush would have been to again tell the wrong stories, maybe even manipulate or communicate by impact – all maladaptive coping mechanisms that I relied on for many years.

I have a tough relationship with immediacy. I've often poured all of my thoughts and feelings onto paper and fired them off to the world quickly. I published each of my first two collections in under a month from start to finish. They read that way, too – hurried, unfiltered, and in my opinion, unpolished – which is why they are no longer in print. In my mind's eye, they were imitations of vulnerability, carefully crafted to project a certain image rather than a reality. They also reflected my limited understanding of my condition. I was still hiding, still afraid of being what I'd been called most of my life: too much.

I was diagnosed with borderline personality disorder during my sophomore year of college. When I presented to clinicians for the first time the year prior, I had been diagnosed with bipolar disorder. I knew immediately that this was incorrect. My saying so further added to the doctors' certainty. People who live with bipolar disorder often don't accept their diagnosis. By protesting the diagnosis, I was confirming it to the people who purported to know best.

Admittedly, I was also initially skeptical of my skepticism. At the time, I was nineteen and in the midst of a deepening crisis, and the people treating me were among the best-trained psychiatric professionals in the world. I felt that I had no right to tell them about myself. I barely knew who that guy really was. All I wanted was for the pain to end, and they promised me it would, so I complied.

To this day, I wish I hadn't. I was pumped full of antipsychotic medications that I didn't need – nine of them in six months – to treat a condition that I didn't have. I often wonder if AstraZeneca sent my psychiatrists to Cabo that year. I became a shell of myself, and still exhibited all of the symptoms I had previously. I was even more emotionally volatile than before, and was struggling to manage myself in a more granular way. I gained fifty pounds in three months, broke out in horrible acne, and could barely muster the energy to get out of bed and go to class. Some days, I didn't even recognize where or who I was.

I often dig my heels in and refuse to let things go. That's more on account of who I am as a person than any diagnosis. I've always been relentlessly stubborn. I was captain of the debate team in high school, and spent four years as a negative speaker. My entire task every time I got up on stage for a round was to prove someone else wrong.

That fall and winter, I got to work doing exactly that. I did as much research as I could on my condition, my symptoms, and other possible explanations for the cluster of symptoms I was exhibiting. I spent hours at a time lost in scientific literature, trying to solve the puzzle of my misfiring brain. By that spring, I was convinced that what I lived with was borderline. My therapist concurred.

I resented that misdiagnosis for many years. In hindsight, the diagnosis tracked with what I'd shared with my treatment team. I had disclosed no trauma history and none of the important emotional context around my suffering. I turned up to their offices exhibiting persistent emotional lability and had been engaging in increasingly impulsive and reckless behaviors well beyond those of my peers. It was a blameless error. They did their best with the information that they had, and I did my best to give them as much information as I could. After all, I was nineteen and had no idea what I was in for.

For a while, I didn't want to accept the reality of what living with borderline would need to look like if I wanted to live a stable and fulfilling life. After I was diagnosed, I wanted nothing more than to be a normal college student. Funnily enough, that desire drove me to avoid doing the one thing that would have made me more "normal": taking it seriously. I didn't possess the skills necessary to manage my condition, and I was lost on trying to learn them. "In order to live a more normal life," my therapist told me, "you need to accept that you will in many ways not live a normal life." More recently, I finally did.

When I began organizing *Diagnostic Features*, I was working toward managing my condition for the first time. It had already stolen much of half of my life from me. I was putting in overtime to maintain the appearance of a well-adjusted individual. There had always been excuses, all of which were quickly stripped away. There's no right time, right moment, to commit to oneself except over and over again forever.

It's occurring to me that I might be a little full of shit here, so let me keep myself honest. I can make all of the excuses in the world, and the truth remains: I have a longstanding fear of being seen. For someone who's shared so many of my most intimate experiences so publicly, I truly didn't want the world or anyone in it to see me as I am. To be emotionally naked before the world is among the scariest things one can do.

Holding back indulged my persistent need to be in control and project that image of a Nice, Well-Adjusted Young Man I'd curated for many years. If I hid enough, I thought, I could maintain the walls I'd built around my true being and prevent the ever-threatening pain of rejection. Ironically, by accepting that the Nice, Well-Adjusted Young Man did not exist, I began to bring him into being.

No mental health condition is easy to live with. A personality disorder is a whole different thing. People hear that word, *borderline*, and they make assumptions. It's a lifelong condition that can be managed and treated, but not cured. Many psychologists and psychiatrists – the very people we expect to help treat mental health conditions – refuse to work with populations living with borderline. It's a highly treatment-resistant condition, and they simply don't think we're worth the time. My therapist of seven years tells me that I'm the only patient of his who lives with this condition and has continued to show up for this long.

Even so, effective treatment options are limited. There's no medication for borderline that does anything more than address symptoms. There's one very particular type of therapeutic treatment – dialectical behavioral therapy – that's been proven to work. Few professionals are trained in it, and it's very expensive to go through. Six months of it ran me over $10,000 out-of-pocket.

Borderline is the thousand-pound elephant I drag around by its neck. It sits at the center of my emotional existence, impacting nearly every part of my life in some way. It doesn't define me, but it certainly shapes me. As it is with many chronic illnesses, managing my condition is often a massive pain in the ass. I was told long ago to avoid disclosing my diagnosis to physicians at all costs, as it could potentially bias their assessments of my physical health. I can't go without sleep, or things deteriorate quickly. I have to consciously monitor my own thoughts and feelings, adjusting and recalibrating in real time. Biting my tongue is a routine and necessary exercise.

When new people enter my life and get closer to me, there's always the tricky matter of disclosure. At one point or another, borderline will always make itself known. All of my friends, save those few who went through the diagnosis with me, have had That Conversation early on in our friendship. As I began to date again, I realized that I needed to disclose my diagnosis to anyone I was seeing before things got serious enough that my condition would impact our relationship. With the publishing of this collection, I suspect that conversation will now need to happen sooner than I'd like with people of all stripes.

While living with a mercurial and intense disposition can be useful, it makes a bunch of very routine things a lot more difficult than they are for most people. There's a reason why many clinicians are of the belief that borderline personality disorder is the most painful mental illness. This sounds like a very borderline thing to say – melodramatic, a little narcissistic, absolute – and I also totally believe it.

To borrow from Marsha Linehan[1], living with borderline is akin to having emotional third-degree burns on 90% of your body. Whenever anyone or anything touches you even slightly, your body's immediate response is to generate the worst and most unbearable pain – a psychosomatic swell of chaos. This is often a legitimate physical sensation that emanates from somewhere in my left abdomen and licks out across my body. I don't think I could ever give words to that feeling, no matter how competent a writer I may be. These poems are my best attempt.

For a while, there was something very shameful-feeling about being a grown man with the free-floating emotions of a teenager. Stigma and shame are inherent to living with a mental health condition. In my case, they're a part of the condition, too. Shame is not a feeling, but a narrative – a chosen story. Once I was able to understand what part of my psyche was stuck, where it was stuck, and why, I was able to begin bringing my emotional functioning more in line with my cognitive self. I began to tell myself more

---

[1] Linehan is credited with developing dialectal behavioral therapy (DBT), the only evidence-based approach proven to treat borderline personality disorder. She lives with the condition, as well.

helpful and accurate stories. That will always be an ongoing process. I get no days off.

There's a noise outside. I'm snatched back from the ether and reminded that I'm running out of time. The clock reads six in the morning, and I'm due downstairs for breakfast in an hour. I take a minute to watch the sun crawl further toward the tree line.

Years ago, I discovered that I tend to attach to place as a center of meaning. This attachment runs through all of my non-fiction and much of my poetry. Unlike my emotions, place is more static and totally within my control. For the most part, I choose where I am. I've also traveled quite a bit these past few years and have stayed in all sorts of places in different corners of the country. That shows in my work.

I think of this as I sit here, stacks of my emotional catalog spread out across this hardwood table, shifting as the morning breeze blows through a crack in the window. I've paced this hotel room for hours, reading the poems out loud, working out exactly what to say. I have a near-pathological obsession with saying the right thing.

All writers possess a practical narcissism; we share in some part to be seen, and this is by itself not a bad thing. After all, why would any of us share what we have to say if we didn't find it important, even if only to us? But for some time, I felt invisible. I wrote *only* to be seen – or rather, to be seen a certain way.

I've worked hard to be a more honest person. *Diagnostic Features* is a new thing for me – a real attempt at vulnerability and sincerity, the kind I was incapable of until I began to accept my history and myself as I am. It's both my attempt to understand my condition, my life as I've lived it, and to share that experience with the hopes of promoting a deeper understanding of a totally human thing: feelings.

It's my hope that this collection will find its way to the right people, and maybe do for them what others' vulnerability did for me over the years. Feelings and emotions are powerful, intangible things that many of us struggle with in different ways. I've succeeded greatly if I can show one person that it's okay to cry, to love, to experience the full range of emotions life has to offer, and that it's okay to ask for help in managing them. No one should bear the weight of their pains alone.

BPD, CPTSD, OCD, IDK – the human condition is the human condition. Emotions are a universal thing, and for one reason or another, many people are plainly ill-equipped to deal with them. Just because I experience my feelings on steroids almost constantly doesn't make any of the things described in this collection any less relatable to people who don't live with borderline personality disorder. The whole thing is just reality turned up past ten. Love, death, heartbreak, confusion, pain, anger, and loneliness – all of these things come with being a person. Feeling things is the price we pay for being alive. None of us makes it out without scars and burn marks.

I promised myself back in my bedroom in Brighton a few years ago that I wouldn't share this collection until it was truly ready – that is, until I was well on my way to being a different person and had begun to jettison my oldest ways of being. Now, here, in this well-appointed hotel room in the Carolina greens, with my poems, I can see myself more clearly than ever before, and I know it's time. I'm at long last ready to throw open the church doors of my being, however intense and scary and new it may be. There is no other way to live well than to live honestly. For once, I'm taking my own advice.

I wondered how you would react when I revealed to you my hidden parts, my ugly parts that don't do well in the sunlight.

Ashley Berry, *Separate Things: A Memoir*

1. Frantic efforts to avoid real or imagined abandonment.

I HAVE THE NERVOUS SYSTEM OF A COMBAT VETERAN patrolling the streets of a faraway place that his children cannot name. The aftershocks of trauma live in our bodies long after the thing itself reaches its end. Mine rolled on for many years, all as I refused to call it what it was. The combat metaphor feels apropos; there's growing debate around whether borderline is its own diagnosis or rather complex post-traumatic stress disorder by another name.

The most widely accepted theory regarding the origins of borderline posits that like all personality disorders, it develops as a result of some sort of childhood interruption – abuse, poor attachment, et cetera – coupled with biological vulnerabilities present at birth. This context should inform your understanding of the condition: not nature, not nurture, but both.

Left to its own devices, the borderline brain operates from a place of fear and insecurity. Issues with identity and negative experiences in early interpersonal relationships fester at the core of this terror. The majority of us who live with borderline experienced inconsistent or hostile caregiving as children, or another form of abuse – physical, sexual, emotional, et cetera. This makes it very hard to

15

trust others, form secure relationships, and let people in.

I'd argue that no single set of symptoms is as chronic and damaging as the difficulties the condition causes in relationships of all kinds. People who live with borderline live in a near-constant state of fear and distrust. Most, I believe, are as totally in the dark about this as I was. It's an exhausting way to live, and it inhibits real connection. It's true that everyone will eventually be taken advantage of in some way, and being a little guarded against con artists and scumbags and dagger-wielders is a wise way to live. But to live with a borderline brain is to believe that there is real, true, fight-or-flight danger in nearly every person you meet – especially those you care about.

Borderline relational functioning is ruled by a disorganized attachment style – a flux between the two most widely recognized types of insecure attachment. Anxious attachment is defined by a deep fear of abandonment in relationships, and a constant need for a type of reassurance that's never enough. At the opposite end of the insecure attachment spectrum is avoidant attachment. As the name implies, people who struggle with avoidant attachment avoid the kind of closeness that an anxious person would crave. They keep people at arm's length out of a deep fear of losing themselves and their independence.

That duality – a desire to pull close (anxious) and a desire to run away (avoidant) – is inherently confusing, both for the person who experiences it within themselves and the people around them. When people got close to me, I did everything in my power to push them away. When they left, I held on for dear life. Borderline is an illness of many such dualities – very ironic, given the black-and-white thinking of the borderline brain. Holding two truths in stasis is not exactly something that people living with borderline are known to be good at.

Frantic efforts to avoid abandonment, real or imagined, are an attempt to balance the first half of that equation. Disordered attachment is never a healthy thing, but when this pattern of behavior plays out in an otherwise secure interpersonal relationship – when no "abandonment" is imminent – it often leads to the exact result it is intended to prevent. If you look hard enough for a reason not to trust someone, you'll almost always find one. If you can't find one, you'll create one.

For much of my life, attempts to avoid abandonment were an unfortunate feature of my friendships, family dynamics, romantic relationships, and professional connections. Minor disagreements, unintentional miscommunications, and misunderstandings were triggers. The slightest indication of an impending "leaving" was enough to short-circuit my borderline brain. "Abandonment" doesn't just occur when someone walks away. This pattern played out whenever I began feeling emotionally abandoned, left to suffer alone. The borderline brain is not adept at suffering alone. It's a misery that loves company.

Relinquishing attachment is a difficult practice, with or without a personality disorder. We've been attempting this as a species for thousands of years. It was the Buddha who said that suffering is born of attachment. Pain is not optional, but suffering is not mandatory. If we're caught up in holding onto people, ideas, and things, we doom ourselves to a deeper kind of pain: the pain of hanging on. Change and loss are both constant things. Accepting this makes it easier to process the pain they bring with them.

Healthy love for others has very little to do with feelings. Infatuation, lust, desire, yearning, and want are feelings. Love is not. It's an intentional, repetitive choice – looking at the world and another person and saying, "I'm doing this thing, embarking on the project of living, and I want to do it with you." It's not a thing rooted in fear; quite the opposite. To attempt to love another person in any capacity is to take a leap of faith over and over again, in *spite* of your fears.

It's true that you can't love someone until you love yourself, no matter how you're trying to love them. I resented that mindset for a long time. Whenever anyone said "you can't love someone else until you love yourself," I interpreted it as saying something about *me*: that I was fundamentally unlovable until I won the war I was fighting with my psyche. I spent much of my life resigned to the fact that said war would never relent. How wrong I was.

Mine was a very limited view of what people actually mean when they repeat that pithy expression. No one needs to be perfect to be loved, but they do need to be somewhat secure, or that love will have nowhere to attach to. To love someone is to risk losing them. The best ending of any kind of love – friendship, kinship, romance – is that one person eventually dies, leaving the other to see it through alone. When the best-case scenario is the ultimate unknown, we're left with no choice but to trust the hairy order of things. That begins with building a deep trust in ourselves.

The poems in this section are indeed "love" poems, in that many of them are about people whom I cared for in an intense way. They do not, however, describe love so much as they do a fear of missing out on it. Each of them represents the swell of terrible dread that washed over my brain as I began to fear that someone was about to walk away (or, in many cases, as they *did* walk away). For a long while, I forgot that I existed when my existence was not being validated by someone else's gaze. After much time alone, I've begun to teach my nervous system that solitude is nothing to be afraid of. It's made my relationships with others and myself much healthier.

Space for Us

I will travel west to the end to find empty space for us
in the stripped-down valley where the land is nude
& vacant, mirror image of your eyes.
The resolute delusions I've built in my rambling mind
will carry us out to San Francisco, where we will settle
somewhere near the center of the best place, almost like
we're at last a part of something.
There is a thing about you that is a newer tragedy,
a fresher distance, & I can hear the silence it excavates
into your cramped room. I will bring you back to me
& we will make our escape, you from your father
& me from my aching. We will make something new
in an old place, like Durgin Park, where I found myself
looking for you in the faces on the bank posters
like you were wanted by an authority we cannot name.
What do you say about us at the mess hall, the barber,
the practice rooms? Who hurt you in it? Who made you
this kind of sad woman? Your old man is a noxious fellow,
a real bastard, & he comes by his vicious tongue honestly.
These things are utterly genetic. We can discuss this
on our drive west, I promise it. We will have plenty of space
for us & our most soured things.

Birthday

It was someone's birthday & I lay there
   listening to the anxious movement through the wall –
   two inconsiderate coeds rolling late into the night,
   twisted in each other, uncovering their natures,

   & I lay there in my own set of new losings,
     each worst of all a set of sorrows,
   calling on the winter to do something fresh,

   at once a wailing, impatience, & then nothing –
   the coeds dead quiet, the stage door slamming.
   There are moments that move too much,

   & I, still in there, bitter in my solitude,
   pushing myself up to close the window
   & let the cracks aging in my small cortex
     lie under the weight of my resentment

Mammogram

There were several words about a potent kind of cancer
       marching through your body as we sat for dinner,
& out of nowhere you asked me to have at you, like that.
  I liked to think I knew better, if only a little,
& so we remained below the thick concentration of lust,
looking at each other, me at you & you at me,
  in this silence so still it felt a vacuum,
  the room failing & wilting, switching a shade of yellow,
& now it's all small ants on a sand dune
  in the middle of a forgotten time

Attachment

Each morning I tread deeper into the shaming,
& I collect the reticence from behind your frames –
that, or I am folding you into an invisible paper crane

All so much, the pre-summer fog collecting on the harbor,
the drip washing the odor of this out of my clothes,
which makes me wonder, *Does anyone dream anymore,
or is it all just empty space between the wars?*

Whoever did that to you, I'll beat them into oblivion
with the bats I used on myself, fully commit
to knocking them over side-silly.   I am in the reeds,
listening for a hint of awe, catching a groan in its echoes

Isolation

Frailest season & the smallest wind
together make these days feel like my first bus ride,
kiss, or those final days as a Catholic
a little less than holiest in doubt
more weighty than thirty silver

One of the attendants tells again of that horror:
Your mind can make anything real
& I have come to know that mine
is the wisest kind of liar

The Houseparty

You hurt most when I want to pull you close to me,
    right as the moon hits mid-night above
    as we slink around each other in the hall,
      pitching longings for interpretation
        as if arguing ethics, stale rubrics,
human honesty, white eyes & Absolute,
        careful around the spilled Keystone,
& you & I make this paltry contact,
      a chance touching of arms,
& my eyes slide sideways & there you are,
   smiling, & I hear it again,
   the cracking of this thing,
   a tetchy splitting sound out the window,
   clean as crystal church bells

Midwinter

If I am to believe you, there is a time in another place
    where we could make a full thing for ourselves,
    retreat into the grooves of a good life, imagined as such,
    looser than this brusque concoction we've wrought,
    the stale days, all of the showy hiding,   & yet
    in this impossible short breath we are in our own worlds,
    orbiting the same sad sun all February long

Third Phase

Call it a small, dying fanaticism, call it headway
Call it   I am grasping at the last bits of this
               still poking out of the long summer

I have a good name, rolls off the tongue,
you say aside to me from beyond the inner wall,

& *Yes*, I chip back, as the syllables hang from my lip
as if you are a violent word, vicious insult, off-limits

I lay here with the Rottweiler, our sightline meeting,
& I whisper to him, *Am I insane?*

A question to which he cocks his head, as if to say,
You tell me.

Scabs

Swallow the thought that this order of love
  is a paper cut you salve until it heals over,
& while you peck the scar we go taunt & sticky
  the tabby swats at the mirror on the door.
Meanwhile I am forcing myself to rewind a video cassette
  with a pencil or, more-so, unbolt a safe door held up
  by Philips heads with a screwdriver.
You push harder, torque it & as the door falls off
  we see a twelfth birthday party inside.
You look at it as if it was something big, or again,
  maybe you just you look at it, I can't tell,
& I shark into my cuts, tending to the gaping wounds
  I've unwound into the center of our saddening thing

Five O'Clock

...the sky still blotting behind the curtains
& I awake, I breathing, I feeling, I undead

know that if there were one truthful thing
I could tell you, it would not be that I am sorry,

though I am, or the way the morning crashes
into the room, as it does, fragmented & shying

Instead that I am grossly ill, that the fire
in my stomach is licking its way up the walls

that someone has taken the blowtorch
& taken all of the gasoline

& I am holding the pack of matches
   in my tremor-wrought hands

California & Montgomery

Alone hotel room in the dead center of empty weekend
  deadened San Francisco, clothing on the floor,
  dirty dishes on the carpet,
& as I gaze out at my saddest city, bridgelight flooded,
  long & upwards at the Bank of America Building,
  I sense that run-down thought finding its way to me,
& so I go down to the bar & I ask for the special with gusto,
  take it down & enter into the nighttime at California
  & Montgomery, the foot of the streetcar rampings
to find my stillness somewhere in this strangest place

Intuitions

Hanging on is a lost art form, a weaving or wine,
   & in this sidelight there's something non-rational,
      not enough to know it, just to catch a hurried look
      as you glitz into the room all flow-like, slip hanging,
      window glow of this late hour lounging momentary
      just long enough to stare dead into the middle of it
      as you crawl into your bed & I slide you my way,
      & from nowhere I feel the stiffening weight of a thing
      I cannot guess around, so I shelve it & choose to muse
      on a sigh, slow heave of your chest, a flickering thing
      I will think out as I maze home, letting it shimmer
      out into the chainsaw Frigidaire hum morning

Book of Worries

Despite my talking, you do not know what I am thinking.
    On my walk along the whipping embankment
    I watch the wake & imagine a few fictions.
                This is the strangest thing, really,
& I laugh to it, but I've sold myself down this river
    for less, which is what I attempt to say in my
    unending deflections.
                I cannot speak up on it now,
    that omen that cradles itself inside me, a kind of
    schoolyard secret, the landmine that falls between us
    as we lie apart in bed, you struggling not to fall asleep
    in your sweaty amber & me running my fingers
    through the knots in your hair,
& so yes I hold my tongue, twirl your ends,
    wondering, wanting, waiting

First line after "For Grace, After A Party"
by Frank O'Hara (1926-1966)

Meditation on *La Gitana*

Cruel fog-like drift out the window trailing down low
around the widow watches, steam press ventilators,
beneath this involuntary azure Newport morning
on which I stroll Broadway & wonder a little bit about you.
I don't know, really, & for once I am meditating
on something very benign, very cool, a little nerve-making.
I think of you under the muddy light of the Gardner,
admiring Kronberg's *La Gitana,* which now that I think of it
reminds me a bit of you if only because it's human divine,
& I do not know if Kronberg knew what he was doing,
but I would like to be convinced.
                                Suspicion tells me
that Kronberg did not intend to frame you,
& that maybe if he saw the way you lamp up in my room,
he'd be struck by it too, almost morose in knowing
there are realities that paintings cannot take down,
that the raw deal outguns, such as a cup of fresh coffee
or a long seasoned thing by the window at sunset,
or maybe a way of walking that cannot be suspended in oil,
or maybe even *La Gitana*.
                All of this longing drives me up my walls
straight to the moulding.   I find things in the roadway
& clutch them, just like how Kronberg clutched his brush!
My words, your words, silly things, don't mean nothing,
& I'm always saying something else, anyways,
never something close.

Detachment

Faraway there is a self-knowing & I am tempted to chase it;
my worst sword is my ever-craving,
& though my intellect cannot make narrative of breezes,
it performs an impossible calculus on my condition,
a pointless heady task that wears on my callouses
An understanding is impossible in its midst,
& so I work it all the way down until the doubt quells,
running my hands along the bannister,
feeling at the impossible colossus in my chest,
the things I carry in my knapsack,
the autumn growing out my window,
                                    & I notice it –
some boulder shifting inside my hard parts,
& a movement begins through the seasons of my being,
all the way this time, & I am slowly surrendering
to the order of things, the pasty tar of human experience,
guessing at the words in the weedy undergrowth
in my heart & the starry thing at its core

2. A pattern of unstable and intense interpersonal relationships characterized by alternating between extremes of idealization and devaluation.

I'M AN INTENSE PERSON, and that's not everyone's favorite flavor of life. I've come to more readily accept that about myself while reining in its wilder expressions. I believe that I'd be at least a little bit eccentric even without a personality disorder. That isn't in and of itself something I dislike about who I am – quite the opposite.

Relationships are always complex and laborious. Anyone who tells you otherwise has never been in one. Borderline makes the task of forming and maintaining them all the more difficult. The cause of this difficulty is the inner conflict discussed in the previous section: the push and pull between the fear of abandonment and the fear of engulfment (being consumed by another person). This often results in people with borderline sabotaging our closest relationships when people get a little *too* close.

The desire for distance – the latter half of that tense equation – often leads me to a place of total detachment and apathy towards closeness, if not an outright rejection of it. This is a dangerous place, one in which I'm most likely to pick fights and engage in extreme self-sabotaging behaviors. The people I loved the most were often on the receiving end of my worst behavior – not because I didn't love them, but because I feared them.

The way people who live with borderline interact with others in relationships is in some ways child-like, lacking the fully developed emotional insight that healthy adult relationships require. Many people who live with borderline, myself included, experienced an event in their developmental phase that was so significant and posed such a challenge to their natural development that it permanently altered them. That is the original wound.

People living with borderline have a tendency to think and act in extremes. This can be a difficult thing for me to understand when I'm emotionally activated. I care a lot about everything, and teasing out what level of that care is personality and what level is disorder is a very involved process that requires a lot of self-awareness and even more practice. Make no mistake – I'm more than alright caring. It often feels like everyone nowadays makes such a show out of not caring that extends well beyond measured detachment. In a world that encourages apathy and disconnect, mere existence over living, giving a fuck about *anything* or *anyone* is a really brave thing to do.

When it came to my relationships, however, I wasn't caring about people – at least not in the way we *ought* to care about other people. My condition blinded me to exactly how much I was taking from others in an attempt to get my needs met. Intensity early on in my relationships (both platonic and romantic) always felt like love. It was really idealization, the cheapest knock-off. I carried this unspoken, unthought belief that if I found the right person or people, they would fill the hole that existed in my being. That's not love; that's using.

Given their size, it's not uncommon for me to misread my own feelings, especially about other people. Limerence and infatuation and love are not emotional equals, but to the borderline mind, they often *feel* the same. I often joke with my friends that I've fallen in love with people I've never spoken to on public transportation, and it's only sort of hyperbole because it all *felt* like the same feeling. I loved the idea of love, but the real thing proved elusive.

This isn't just a struggle that people with borderline face in the context of romantic relationships. I misjudge the closeness of platonic relationships, too. Parsing out my own feelings about attraction and desire and friendship can be challenging. My emotions often overpowered my reason, leading me to embarrassing places. My heart was the thing I stabbed my brain with.

The other extreme, devaluation, is often an unconscious coping mechanism. It allows emotionally traumatized people to easily discard meaningful relationships without dealing with the painful after-effects of someone walking away. If the person doing the "abandoning" is evil and sucks and isn't worth all that much to you, their loss is a little easier to take – until it isn't.

The process of swinging between these two poles is known as splitting. This is but one of many defense mechanisms employed by the borderline mind to cope with instability. I've torched a lot of relationships in frantic, unconscious efforts to protect myself from the pain of being engulfed and/or abandoned. It's a confounding behavioral pattern, and it's wildly destructive.

The common perception seems to be that people living with borderline are unaware of the emotional fallout triggered by our behavior, and that all of us seek to avoid any kind of interpersonal accountability. This is sometimes true, especially for people who allow their condition to remain untreated. I was casually cruel to the people I was closest to for many years. It was often easier for me to be kind to strangers than to care for the people closest to me. I picked senseless fights and did senseless things to drive people away. That felt like a far easier pain to bear than watching them leave, or worse: letting them close enough to see the parts of myself that I loathed.

This behavioral pattern broke many of the most important relationships in my life. At my bottom, I was a very lonely young man, and I deserved to be. I was out of control. I was never fully cognizant of the impact my condition had on the people around me until one day I finally was.

In appropriate dosages – when there *is* a real reason – shame and guilt can be healthy emotions. If you do something worthy of guilt, it's a sign of a healthy conscience to feel very bad about it. I behaved very poorly for a long time, and made poor choices that I'd never make again. Once I recognized exactly what my behavior had done to the people around me in a more real way, I was consumed by both for a very long time.

While I changed *for* myself, I began that process because of other people. Sometimes you need to learn a lesson many times for it to stick, even if you'd prefer to have learned it only once. Interpersonal relationships will always require a little more effort for me than they do for most, but accepting that has guided me to healthier ones.

The poems in this section have a deliberate flow to them, one intended to demonstrate the drift between idealization and devaluation. If you look closely enough, you can see a certain kind of changing occurring *in medias res* – the moment when I decided that this was no way to live, no way to treat people, and certainly no way to love.

About Autumn

I suppose it was a kind of love with you, October
  & if you squinted at it wrong it vanished;
  The holocaust of the willows hastened &
  the trees grew naked for your touch,
  all the classic signs to a total dread

I have a well-rehearsed apology, sincere,
from snowbound Halloween weekend,
written sleepless, sweating and tossing about
as I mulled the October, betrayed its secrets,
& let go of every blemished thing

Yearn

In a wake the sky dials down
& finally the day is extinguished

& finally evening falls into it,
    on the cast of the city,

& finally the moon
& finally we settle raw under silk,

    finally tangled up in it, present,
    my hands full of anticipating,

close as a brace of doves

O Woman

O woman who thrashes through the nights,
   crooked anadem, satin slip falling low,
into the mound of things that I conjure up
   as I drift off into a half-resting;

I, broken-jawed, cawing at stars,
   withering at the Maytime bloom,
think to myself of the hostile winter,
   longest months of that love,

& as the rheumatic dead room zips up,
   I think those words through

& let them trail off for the better

Indictment

I've always been porous in this way, as though everything
slips thorough my fat-clumsy fingers as I bobble it
The hair on my arms is almost blonde in the sun now,
& I don't have the fighting insight to flip back

If I look long enough at all the people walking by
in the day, I begin to wish all of me was blonde & thin,
  light enough to walk off into a field of high wheat &
  squirrel away until the dragging storms fly past

When I was younger & stronger than present tense
I told myself it would pass, even if like a kidney stone,
  but I could not trap the thought & hold it after the
  deadening summer got sniffing at it

What else is there to say on it but that?
It's a small thought; we can watch it grow together,
or I can sit here on the edge of the Harbor, rocking
in the breeze, awaiting the judgements of the universe

Lovebirds

Between skyscrapers & analog antennae
above the fruited hot tar streetscapes

all of my thought appears mad loud
in between low-strung cloud cover

& I am treading closer to it, dagger in hand,
caressing & teasing it all raw and fine-like

I want to fly like doves close to the Sun,
against the rotten record of it

The draw is overlarge, still, not quite

************, Sunset, October

I will split you until I no longer
recognize the sum of what you were

until I seek dreams & you are wading
in the colors of a slipping unreality

I will reimburse you with fire
I will douse you in my untrust

& you will slip through my palms
    in a slow melt of ice

Epiphany

I recognize your presence in this,
      playful love, the thing you gestured at

I think of you & of this crooked closing,
& I know the core of it, the black roses,

    the sad candor in your dancing
        dull tremor in your voice

See the dissonance now?
Almost like wild roses without thorns,
& such a thing is not for us in this life

If & When

We both lit up & stood there, & I, already at
a dizzying height, saw you in your highest form

& as we watched each other down for that lucid second
    as I chewed on my Camel I began to believe in you,

    the way a child believes in Santa, a nun in Christ,
    beyond the sort of faith any of us should bear,

        the way anyone can believe if they try, but
none of us ever do, so if & when, if I am blessed,

I should want to try with you

Vignette View of You & William Blake

I find you reading Blake beneath a weeping willow,
  tucking your hair back behind the temple tips
  of your eyeglasses, surrounded by the fronds

I take my time to kneel at the base of the leaning tree,
  arm steadying me against the hardened dirt, kick out
  my legs & I say *I will sit & read with you*

& we will smoke the headiest stuff, stare off
  at the suntowers, be so very anchor present

  in the warm moment, wasting away
  the trancing afternoon together

May

Beneath the sagging oak I sit & think about
      all of your spellbinding, & how maybe

        if we really tried we could make
        return to the old ways

If life were a fair exercise, all these bodies
      would reanimate

& the dead would fall down the middle
      of a blank Fifth Avenue

Our visions would go ablaze
& we would slide across the pavement

lock looks & lose ourselves
in the thicker bits of each other

New Year's

Couldn't say it. Words got caught somewhere
                inside my black lungs
You dressed in your dazzling clothes
You dressed in your feel-good clothes
The whole of the television room filled with
     your fascinating kind of sanctuary
The quiet grace of a woman on her way, & o
     how I saw it – the charming things,
     the speckles of fantastic irreverence,
quietly wilting under the weight of your prologues,
& in that simple second we were at the center
of an impossible universe, in which I would have spun
until it collapsed upon itself

After "Bird Understander"
by Craig Arnold (1967-2009)

49

Letter to Sarah

Sarah if there is light in California, let it shine tonight
      if the sun comes up, let it sing to you in sighs

We are all stuck in these trenches, lonely for life
      amid an abundance of dying

We are all no good at things which demand clarity
      so I speak in my sticky ambiguities & poems

I think of you always, especially under the rains,
     even as the years pass & we all build our own silos

To be a friend is to live with a constant softening
To love is to love is to love.   To continue with it

is a fitful thing, bizarre almost.   I get the sense
the strange vibrating, & know it will live forever

For Sarah D, with love

Plymouth, July 6th, 4:45 AM

Same feeling as ever, a lamblike thought,
     frill-less you on which I edge my dulling brain
I will grip this moment between my fingers,
     taste it & make motions of acceptance –
     You look good in this light, you say to me,
& I do not protest but turn a simple phrase, *You too,*
  as I remember that insecurity is another man's currency,
  no good here in this locked room where we shift around,
  tendering ourselves comfortable in silence,
  the field crickets warbling out the screen.
  I tuck my arm into yours, sliding us around,
 & we dive into it – a momentary blessing, nothing more

Transatlantic Red-Eye, Boston to London

This never-ending daylight gives you a pale.
Your head thrown back, your mouth in a gasp,
certainly not *Cosmopolitan*-like but nevertheless
in a way very beautiful in that it is stillest you
& for a minute I wonder if we've gone all sixteen again,
me totally in the woods on your love, unthinking,
you & your sanctifying stuff, distilled to its root.
I go for your hand, nails ripped to jagged bits,
lost in my own wonder in the jet stream,
just simply   lost in my own wonder.
While I am never one to be at peace,
         you are never one to doubt it

Curlew

Midday coming over the far cut
& I, still affixing, ground my feet
in the harder sand, plying it into mounds
This is a Plutoish place, you know,
desolate & slimy, & I find myself deliberating
a more favorite outcome in which I am a better,
stronger man   in which I clench my fists
& shatter the glass, look at the reflection
through the blood in my mouth, say to you,
I really did a number this time, didn't I?

At the Metropolitan Ballet

I want to be Frank O'Hara longing after Vincent Warren
  from the pews of the old hall on 55th Street,
    except it is me 'n you at Baker's or under football neon
  at my bar, joying in the suncast at Haight & Waller.
  In it's place I will take an evening ambling aimless,
  small talk & palms sweaty & hair wilding around
  as the grackle is trying to cough something up,
  or tell you that I am a little nervous as a patient is
  because the size of my things is larger, headier
  than I would care to admit to someone lighter than me.
Nowadays I see nothing beyond what maybe I can touch,
  a queer practice when that rotted space was always loud.
Maybe just some small thing, a small want, it's fine,
  I have many, like seeing Spain or tumbling drunk
  through London with the poets, the puffing hydrangeas
  in the flower box or the few humless moments,
  watching the whitecaps break at the rocks in Aquinnah,
  or laying in bed with you until the last morning light,
  most of which are nothing & yet

Durham

Tonight there is a light flickering in the corner
    of the most sacred room in this old hotel
    above the armchair in which I sit with my collection
    of worries, which were always going to torch me,
    & I can infer by now in this night that you have yours,
    or maybe my silly little sideways brain is making
    spectacle of you & your light mysteriousness.

Don't you know you are but a small mystery?
Not because you are lying, but be honest –
    we all dance through our opaque worlds,
    totally unknowable beyond unflinching trust
    which is the most difficult blue task for me,
    though I do not find you terribly difficult, but soft,
    like the way your pupils sprite wide as you look at me,
    which does something quite nice & unexpected
    to my insides like a relief or Bulleit 'n a slice
    of May lemon or the sound of roiling thunder

Maybe you do not need this light, as in maybe
        it is really my bag of imaginary stories,
        & I can grin and bear that embarrassment
          of a misread message in a bottle, forget it,
        & still I will leave on the light tonight,
          a kind of vigil for your gone world

3. Identity disturbance: markedly and persistently unstable self-image or sense of self.

I'VE BEEN A MILLION DIFFERENT MEN in my lifetime, each different than the last. Growing up, I believed that I was simply an eccentric person with a wide variety of interests. I changed my style frequently. I picked up as many hobbies as one could for no longer than a day. My interests changed quickly, as did many other aspects of my personality. I couldn't decide who I was, no matter how tirelessly I tried. I was going to be a librarian, and then an architect, and then a musician and an attorney or politician or a philosophy professor or a forever student.

Transience of desire is, of course, very normal for children and adolescents. Ask a child what they want to be or do and they'll tell you whatever they feel like telling you on that given day. Their tastes and preferences are subject to their whims. This becomes more of a pathology, however, when the pattern continues into adulthood and it permeates every aspect of one's life.

When dealing with chaotic or abusive environments, a child does what they must to survive. Shapeshifting is a survival mechanism, fueled by the belief that if only you could be the right version of yourself, someone will stick around and love you. To live with borderline is to frequently look in the mirror and be greeted by a face you can't truly recognize because it remains ever-changing.

This phenomenon isn't limited to the so-called afflicted. After all, next to no one is real nowadays. So many people are lost in the routine act of mask-making. The Culture almost demands it from us. We hide behind our screens and fast fashion. We're encouraged to live our lives dead from the neck up. Instagram is always trying to sell us something. Podcasts try to tell us what we should say to attract people. We're always being told who to be and what to like. If you aren't careful about what you consume, it consumes you.

Oftentimes, people who live with borderline define ourselves relationally. When you struggle to identify who you are, it's very easy to get totally lost in other people. We unconsciously assume the traits of those with whom we desire closeness. I've noticed it in myself many times. Without recognizing it, I became a different person around different people. If I wanted to be liked, I made myself likable to whoever it was I wanted to like me.

I have a bad habit of refusing to ask for what I need to keep the peace. Often, I found that my fear of abandonment led me to avoid difficult conversations. If you're always taught that your needs are too much, you eventually give up on asking for others to meet them. In time, this turns into prioritizing the needs of others over your own. I've learned that you always need to ask, because if you don't, they'll force themselves out, typically in the most passive-aggressive ways imaginable.

A big part of struggling with borderline is having a baseline emotional state that is well above "normal" (see Criterion 6). This in and of itself makes developing a stable identity remarkably difficult for people living with borderline. Our feelings about things and people can vary greatly with our mood. I'm constantly working to discern my true beliefs about myself and the world from my transient feelings.

"Discovering yourself" is pitched to us as a core part of your late teens and twenties. I think this is wrong, only in that it's very condescending and lacking in self-awareness to suggest that this is a thing only young people need to do. Self-discovery is a lifelong task. We all need to engage in it regularly, lest we lose the best things about ourselves to the acts of mask-making and wall-building.

Towards the end of my undergraduate studies, I was taken by existentialism, a patchwork of philosophical beliefs that interrogate authenticity and what it means to be a human being. It came to me at an odd time. My senior spring, I loaded up on philosophy courses, including one with my college advisor on existentialist philosophers. It was a genuine interest of mine, so I found it very easy to engage with the material. That semester was cut short by the pandemic; I chuckled a bit when I logged into my first Zoom class to discuss Albert Camus' *The Plague*.

Central to existentialism is the idea of 'being' – how identity and purpose are formed and shaped over time. Human beings are unique in that we don't have the same defined essence as objects or animals. To borrow from José Ortega, instead of being given a purpose, human beings have to "be [ourselves] in spite of unfavorable circumstances" and "make [our] own existence at every single moment.[1]" We must conceptualize and "attempt to carry out a program or project of existence.[2]" Borderline or

---

[1] Ortega y Gasset, José. (1941). Man has No Nature. In H. Weyl, E. Clark, and W. Atkinson (Trans.). *Historia como sistema* (p. 153)

[2] Ibid, p. 154.

not, we're all doing the difficult work of making ourselves. Feeling a little lost at times is a part of that process.

Like all facets of borderline, being a little more willing than most to shape-shift has its benefits. I've been told I make people feel included in group settings, something I take a bit of pride in. My ability to pour my all into any new thing has allowed me to excel at several different careers now, including ones I never thought I'd pursue. My condition has also allowed me the opportunity to be many different people, all as myself. I feel no need to box myself into one way of being. I've kept some parts of all those people inside me.

One of the only things I've consistently wanted to do in every frame of my life has been to write. Writing has served as a bowline for the rest of my often unstable and ill-defined sense of self. I was a writer at twelve, at fifteen, at 20, and now 27, almost 28. My body failed me, and my mind failed me, but writing never failed me. It's been my North Star of being over the past fifteen years, even as everything else fell apart and came back together. No matter how I feel or where I am or what I do, I'm a writer.

These past few years, I've spent a lot of time alone in an effort to get to know myself, what I want, and what I really *need* for myself – to engage in the long, messy project of making *me*. I work to meet that man every moment of every day. I get the sense it took me a bit longer than many to realize this. It was well worth the wait.

I quite like who I've been making, and I will continue to make him as I want him to be. I love and cherish him now more than ever before. These poems chronicle the work I've done to get there.

Buffalo, New York

I am fourteen & I am in Buffalo for the night
at canyon cavern hour, when my words dance
in a small universe of the unfamiliar
until I open my eyes & like a fixed set of dice
fall squarely into dreams of being someone new

David Rakoff, Canada, August 17th, 2012

He was playing Sigmund Freud in a
Christmas display window at Barney's

David, gently asking leading general questions –
        "Why do you think you said that?"

It was both public & intimate
All the time, everything, chemical,

a low rumbling, a vague buzz,
                        an olfactory insult

For those few moments we were singing,
our drunkenness was twofold

The chamber opens up & enfolds that name,
                        & you keep it.

Found poem from "Our Friend David,"
a special by This American Life

Everyone

Here, I am everyone
I lose myself in it

& chase the morning heron for her word
I leave behind a shadow for the taking

& vanish into the underbrush

Inside

Everything coming up burlap,
unhanded & overexposed,

so I spend my daylight observing,
waiting for something larger to give,

years & nothing budges

The innocents have murdered
& buried their purity in perfection pills

no one is left to count the dead

Their hearts wail from below the dirt,
ripped out, & I, living among them

Eighth Avenue Local, Sunday Morning

The Eighth Avenue Local
    vaulting under slimy New York,

      & I inventory the scene – snack peddler,
        two rabbis, everyone sideswaying.

"This is where good people come to live,"
    a mother says to her child.

I am unsure, & I do not well-wear a poker face.
She gives me a look & I am convinced.

Some Days

Saw it first out back on one of the cold days,
       wasting evening in early November

The kids played in the window next door
       one of them put his hands to the glass

             flailing around the three-season porch,
             his arms outstretched for something,

             the slow snow wagging its way down
             through dry nighttime, none of it
             caught his eye except the fuming Red,
             & so he stopped his dance

             & watched as I yanked at the filter
               We caught each other's glances

             & conferenced on boyish innocence
             & the space between

After 'Starling'
by Richard Kenney (1948-)

Introductory Questions

Someone asked me if I believe in God
& I thought quietly to myself & not her,

I'm slow to believe in anything past morning,

instead of my cynical bite, I crushed my tongue
& smiled all shy behind my many maskings,
toothy as ever, frozen in a quick function,
looking her up & down & up again;

she was staring hard & so I whimpered
in defeat & said,   *Yes, I do believe.*

Dead Winter

Dead winter attacks, long winter,
sacred winter of brokenness in which
I attempt to mutter my silent prayers
as the macadam ices over the roadlines
& I hold my hand to the shift & tip the pedal
& somewhere you hold my heart in your gums
    You say all coy, *Are there ghosts here?*
I have said that there are ghosts everywhere,
& so I say to no one, *This place is a place, darling,*
& I swerve to avoid the highway junk,
    my grip tightens as the ice slushes
& I sit in alienating quiet as the old road
    drags me up home

After "Dog Autumn"
by Choi Seung-ja (1952-)

St. Valentine's Day

If I were of this earth, I'd be a lark
    singing through the grapevines

But there is something between myself & I,
        more than space or time

A one-sided longing for a fuller man

In my mouth is a bag of glass marbles
                on which I am always choking

    my mouth runs like a motorboat
    my mouth runs like a river

Man at 9th & Irving

Waiting for the trolley in smelly bus shelter
   & this man, hair buzzed to his scalp & his tee shirt
   hanging off his shoulders, sort of like a dirty dress,
   & even as I sweat out booze, short on conversation
   he looks to me & asks me about golf at Harding Park,
   & I smile at him & he says, straight-faced, so serious,

   Maybe I will see you at Harding Park. Do you golf
   at Harding Park? If so, maybe we will golf at Harding Park,

   & I see him smiling & waiting & so I say, half-truth,
   Yes, maybe we will golf at Harding Park.

Diagnostic Features

I seek myself in the gutter trashes, small reflections
       the size of an eyelash, floating down Comm Avenue
       into the grates as I begin asking the questions
       I have written on flashcards in my mind.
There are things that live inside the walls of my softer sides,
               longings for a disparate time.
       The coiled progression plays itself again on the piano
in my living room, one note at a time, right down to the last
sticky key.   In time, I will again forget
most of my history, like many things, except the feeling,
which always has a way of sitting raw & childlike
in my abdomen, against the stapled crate of things
I am working to unbox & put back in their ordinary places.
If I were not this way, I would be another thing entirely,
almost a circus complete with peanuts.   I will not lather
myself in it,   as somewhere a window is waiting to be lit
into a comely state that feels more earthy, more serene
in the way it laps the pond, both slow & not,
but definitely in a kind of motion.   I will get to thinking
on it, the knowing, the slowing of spirit, that way in which
I will drape my colds, the things I'd wish to leave behind, in
the brightest wallflowers my imagination can hold.

Equinox

Grief is the thing that questions,
  browning things in the garden,

busting out from the crooked stairs
  another weed, another moment

Somewhere in the city there is
  a grown child with a want, a need,

& somewhere in his head
  is the idea that he should take it

maybe snuff it, maybe hold it,
  never share it, whisper it

to the imaginary friends he's made
  floating in the foothills,

bounding onto the subway,
  the conga line & for a minute

I chew it, the thought of freeing,
  put my lips up under my teeth

the way I do when I'm keeping a secret,
  unable to digest the mineral additive

of stenchy guessing as my system
  cannot tolerate it, & so I let go

of the thought & I still see
  the child, hear him laughing,

  & know the world is for both of us

Perfect Because

I am perfect in most of all my imperfections –
    the scars in my cruxes,
    beauty mark, snaggle tooth,
    thinning hair or how my mouth tenses
    as I lift two weights from a busted nerve
We are all charged with our damages,
    all covered in love,
wearing our stories that tell themselves

4. Impulsivity in at least two areas that are potentially self-damaging (e.g., spending, sex, substance abuse, reckless driving, binge eating).

WE'RE A RECKLESS PEOPLE. We drink too many beers, smoke too many cigarettes, play a little fast and loose with promiscuity and other "regular" norm-defying behaviors. Recklessness is not a unique thing in our time. This tendency becomes pathological within the context of borderline personality disorder when it becomes "self-damaging" – that is, when it has a notable impact on day-to-day functioning. Letting loose isn't necessarily a problem. It becomes one when you lose your ability to reel it in.

I read somewhere that self-destruction is fun until it's not. It was fun for me until it wasn't. In its least regulated state, the borderline mind is prone to rash decision-making with little regard for outcome. As you can imagine, this has gotten me into deep trouble over the years.

People who live with borderline are wired for impulsivity. As with most aspects of the condition, this is due to interactions between our early childhood experiences and biological factors. As children, many of us didn't learn to regulate our emotions to the extent that others did. Further, the fuzzy chemical composition of our brains prevents us from always thinking through the vast array of potential consequences we create for ourselves and others with our choices. Act now, think later is our default setting.

The best way to conceptualize this criterion, and this condition more broadly: within each of us living with borderline, there is a gaping exit wound, a reminder of whatever experience or experiences led to our state of disorder. As we age, the presence of this hole grows larger. As others adjust to adult life, that wound prevents us from doing so. We begin to reach for anything we can to fill it – pills, partners, and Pabsts among them.

I was an impulsive child. It led to much of the trouble I got into at school and at home. I would act carelessly, say things I didn't mean, and take senseless risks with my body and mind. This behavior extended well beyond the kind of impulsivity we expect from children and adolescents. I lacked the ability to think through my decisions clearly, chiefly because my emotions overwhelmed my reason. While this is very normal behavior for young people, it followed me into my adolescence and young adulthood, where it became even more of a problem.

My late teens and early twenties were defined by this kind of unthinking behavior. I would drive my old, beat-up Honda CRV down the iced-over backroads of North Dartmouth until midnight, doing well over ninety miles per hour down a two-lane drag just to feel something. When I got to college, I took to self-destruction quickly. I never saw a bad idea that I didn't want to try on for size. I'll leave some of the wilder *adventures* of my youth to the imagination; vulnerability doesn't always require a public confessional.

Disinhibition – acting without restraint – is a marker of the condition. The lifetime probability of developing a substance use disorder may be as high as 72 percent[1] for people who live with borderline. We're all very unique people, but we're not all that unique in our core challenges. Like many only children, I thought I was special until I realized I wasn't. This is all very borderline stuff.

Drugs and alcohol were readily accessible as soon as I got to college – right when my condition began to worsen. I took to booze like I took to most harmful things, and I kept taking and taking until my body couldn't handle it anymore. There was a period of 72 days between my final two years of undergrad during which I drank half a gallon of table wine a *day* through a straw. I have a fake tooth – I won't tell you which one – as a result of my face slamming into a South Boston curb at the end of a night of heavy drinking. When everything is more intense, more all-or-nothing, it's easy to seek both excitement and relief in accelerants. In my case, it was an ugly thing.

The self-destructive habits of my late teens and early twenties were terrifying to experience, and terrifying for the people in my life to witness. The relationship between art and so-called 'madness' is so beyond cliché, but things become cliché because they're kind of true. The tortured artist thing sounds cool and edgy and fun when you're nineteen and ingesting enough psychoactive substances to anesthetize a small Catholic country. It gets boring and dangerous real fast. By the time I was twenty-one, I couldn't function; I took a semester off to try and right the ship. There was nothing beautiful or romantic about it. It was mostly just sad, and very, very lonely.

---

[1] Tadic A, Wagner S, Hoch J, et al. Gender differences in axis I and axis II comorbidity in patients with borderline personality disorder. Psychopathology. 2009;42:257-263. doi: 10.1159/000224149.

Self-exploration and actualization are normal college experiences, which I had plenty of. Plenty of people drink beer and smoke cigarettes and fall in love. But when behavior deviates from a norm *and* causes significant distress, it becomes pathological. I wasn't experimenting; I was engaging in reckless, self-destructive behavior for no other reason than to feel everything and nothing at all, all at once.

My impulsive behaviors were an attempt to blunt a deep emotional pain. I was using substances to erase the memories of a sordid personal history. I don't believe that it's a coincidence that once I was no longer being abused and exploited as I was for almost a decade of my life, I took to drinking or smoking my way out of having to face the fact that I *was* abused and exploited for almost a decade of my life. I didn't want to acknowledge what that experience did to me, and the things it made me believe about myself and others. Like so many other people who experienced that kind of trauma, I destroyed my body because a part of me felt that *I* deserved to be destroyed. I hated everything about myself. When you hate yourself that thoroughly, it impacts everyone around you.

Actually facing the pain and emptiness has been a much more effective way of coping than trying to drown those feelings and memories altogether. I'm still prone to thoughtlessness and rash decision-making born from momentary emotional impulse. This is less of a coping mechanism than a biological tendency I work hard to resist. I'm more deliberate now, and I'm still prone to unthinking in the way some people are prone to seizures.

Like everyone, I remain a work in progress. That work is far more bearable than it was when I was numb to everything. Numbness can protect us from pain, but it always comes back worse. No amount of fleeting relief is worth that.

Trains

One o'clock paints railroad tracks
on the ceiling filled with trains of mind,

inching across a yard full of dead butts
rat motels engine oil leaky faucets

& hypodermics – white rails on paint,
bubbles & cobweb scars, cat scratches

I notice & then I slide into nothingness,
  wasting off into it at one o'clock

Afternooning

Ten a.m. & the room smells
like pulp rot beer & staling perfume

& the walls are covered in books
day swaddling me as I smell the pulp,

beer & perfume, a heavy reminding.
The bookcase, caught in afternoon Rosedale,

lounging along the agley doorjamb
filled with the ephemera of my youth,

giving me the dirtiest looks,
the gnarliest phrases,

& the room reeking of pulp, beer
& the staling perfume.

Bad Habits

Swigged a shot of it from bottle in the trunk
constellations were grinning in the mirrors

thought on it, & looked just like the whites of yr eyes;
let settle under tongue, let soak rinse repeat

neighbor stumbling, dog crawing, moon rising,
bad habit ingraining, time slowing, liquor soaking,

& forget slow building in the center

American Haiku[2] / Impulses

Hard impulses
Sending me
into a spin

American Haiku / Buying Cigarettes

I go to the store
Blues, ten bucks a pack
smoking away my paycheck

American Haiku / Digits

Ten missed calls
in my phone inbox
asking for me

American Haiku / Sober

No more drugs
I'm going mad –
I can feel it

---

[2] A specific form of haiku devised by American Beat poet Jack
Kerouac (1922-1969). While the traditional Japanese form consists
of three lines with 5, 7 and 5 syllables, respectively, Kerouac's
import doesn't care much for such rigidity.

DeKalb Avenue

Under this dirty motel, the R train kicks dust
    onto the platform & casts rats about,
    rolling to a stop & the train doors glide open
    & a pair of lovers force their way into the car,
    sliding down the skiddy benches
& I, all sad-eyed, watch them rejoice in the trappings of it,
    the emotional window-dressing,
    all of it drowns as the train plunges
    into the other world

Williamsburg

Bitter at 8th & Driggs

stumbling thru headlight glass eyeballs
in the Brooklyn night

Eighteen, wine rushing my veins,
tripping down towards the L alone

My heart tangled tightly in the chainlink fences,
shredded into its finest parts

My somber thoughts flooding Williamsburg,
waiving around until morning

Closet Canticle

Is there a world outside these walls
with you & I between them?

In here, dim light & yr milky tone;
the croaking of the front door,

the older thing wilting, paint ashy
on the windowsill, laying here

as the afternoon winds sing your
small syllables through the vinings

Plum Tree

I divided by zero & ended up
holing out below strobe lights

imagining grief television, poetry,
       lilac wine, rose gardens, magic
      & Jesus, all in my reach,

& still I want to burn, as Hell is no less a fire,
   no more a place than the winning world

6th & Minetta

I stand lonely at 6th & Minetta
  basking in slow October

as soggy cardboard soda cans
  & cracking leaves race towards

the storm drains under the wafts
  of a sad slow smoking day

drifting through hazy skies,
  silky smelly airport dreams,

Con Edison smokestacks
  wafting up from the streets

If the world were 6th & Minetta
  I would be almost as free

as a chicken at the opening
  of the autumn harvest

falling in love at record stores
  smiling, faces, subway cars,

where two men clawed at each other
  & skid across the slush splattered on

the floor, or when I visited
  J's walk-up at 12th & 2nd

where I drank from a handle
  of New Amsterdam straight until

she had to help me walk down

five flights of tenement stairs,

all gentle the way you help a man
    in an hour of unobvious need

I see these things at 6th & Minetta
  where that world is a sick cigarette,

& I am stomping it into the cracks
  in the sidewalk with my heel

as I record store smile &
  crawl into a spinning taxicab

Greyhound, Boston to Newport, Saturday Night

Young woman sits before me tired
  & disc lantern moon falling
  on the busted out mill windows
  beneath colder constellations

I sip at screwdriver in Minute Maid bottle
I think of simple times

I think of heavy city, city of wonder
           city of broken dream

           city of windows
           city of lost souls

A flesh braided in with mine, whoever that is,
  as bus barrels through city of blanket angels
  as bus takes me to the other world

Blood Orange

The long afternoons & the pill bottles
caught a cast of dull light;

Walls went blood orange like wildfires

You would rub glass on your bare knuckles
You would ask why you bled so much

You would get drunk & stick your upper half
                    out of the bedroom window

                    over the alley
                    & play balancing games

You would inhale plaster & cry drunk
            under the low hum of sagging power lines'
                            streetlight buzz

If you'd fallen, nights would've stilled
Instead, bottle-strained light, blood orange

Maverick & Chelsea

At another red light, waiting to cross
as I watch a man drinking ethanol
    from a paper bag

It's lethal, I say, *It'll kill you, you know*

I know, he replies, *All the better*

& he tugs my collar to pull me
    down to his misery & says,

We all die & I choose when

I choose tomorrow so we sit as he drinks
    his methane & I burn my hundreds
    down to nothing

& we laugh at the Gods
    besting them at their own game

    tangled with the fates
    cage matching our way down the block

Benzodiazepines

Would save up pills for the long nights,
        swallow them down to cull the thing

Would spit fire at hollow men, would flame,
        sleep all day, dance all night

Would roll dice, slam drink,
        sink into the bed down to waist & wither

Would write obituaries, fire off rockets,
        taunt ghosts through the night

Would crash cars, torch buildings, fix fights,

Would undo mathematics, taint smiles,
        rebirth, wail, screech, cry

Would come crashing out into empties,
        drag whole rooms into the marshes,

Would cry over stereos, would slap sinners,
        burn Social Security cards, laugh

Would lose bets, would break fasts
Would love,   would lose

Brother

April, floating around the kitchen, & I am watching you
live out the grief as we listen to the sad newspaper sounds

If there is a bottom, we have reached it
                        we are lost in it together now

We have boiled our feelings, bubbled our tears
      pooled them together & sieved them into this

& we wax poetic on Dexter, roasting inside, watching
      the deeper drags curl through the box fan up to the lights

I am sitting on the broken chair, watching, as a painter
      watches the flock of gulls wander the harbor, thinking

how Middle East this all is, the same wasteland,
& you still deny the chance to let your soul breathe lightly

We are in the thick of it now, Brother,
We are in the swampy morass, the thick-cut, the hardening

We are crawling through it into the brilliant thing
      together

For Kai, with endless love

203 Franklin Street

Imagine Cambridge, a warm night
J on the stoop eating European plums
   drunk on Lagavulin or IPAs

The bar's closed down & I'm smoking
                     & J invites himself,
      falls onto the stairs, head gyrating

His mind is stuck at St. Paul's & Auvergne
        & I'm trying to peel him off of it

He is honest, no different than himself

J tells me that his fortunes are coming up
   pitches his novel to me between drags

At once, we're set free in the pastures
               of our minds,

wandering across miles of prickler bushes,
      barefoot, uncertain, serene

For Jesse "Goose" Burkhardt (d. 2022)

North Beach, Sunday Morning

I am lost in the blasted abscess of my mind,
sun pouring down from Oakland, fingers
cranking nervously as the cable car climbs up
Mason Street, jittering the remnants of the evening
like pocket change honey in a jar or maybe
the crankshaft, which sounds to be a hundred or so,
as I am reminded by the crooked day
that nothing is forever, not my wants
& not these shakings, pressure on my temples,
the blistering October sun, the feeling
the word or this western slouching

5. Recurrent suicidal behavior, gestures, or threats, or self-mutilating behavior.

EVEN IN THIS SHOCK AND AWE WORLD of ours, suicide remains an extreme taboo. We're routinely fed videos of extreme acts of violence from the comfort of our bedrooms. Suffering porn is our thing. Even so, suicide remains tucked out of sight until another person dies by it. It's a perplexing thing. The human body is extremely resilient. In its most natural state, it works overtime to adapt as it must to keep us alive. Self-harm and self-annihilation stand in stark contrast to this basic biological truth of sustaining oneself.

Over half of people living with borderline will at some point attempt suicide, and up to ten percent will die by it[1]. Non-suicidal self-harming behavior is also prevalent, with anywhere between 65 and 80% of us engaging in it in some form[2].

---

[1] Paris J. (2019). Suicidality in Borderline Personality Disorder. Medicina (Kaunas, Lithuania), 55(6), 223. https://doi.org/10.3390/medicina55060223

[2] Brickman, L.J., Ammerman, B.A., Look, A.E. et al. (2014). The relationship between non-suicidal self-injury and borderline personality disorder symptoms in a college sample. *Borderline Personality Disorder and Emotion Dysregulation* 1, 14.

There are many things about the condition that provoke these self-destructive tendencies: seeking relief from the grave intensity of our everyday emotional velocities; communicating our feelings by impact; a reaction to the deep shame and guilt that many of us with borderline carry almost constantly. The pressures on our consciousness are unrelenting, and unlike many well-adjusted adults, many of us are unequipped to handle them.

Living with the kind of emotional pain inherent to borderline on a regular basis – feeling the worst you've ever felt each and every time you feel *even kind of bad* – is not something that anyone is supposed to be able to handle. At its worst, it often presents a totally false but terrifying ultimatum: jump from the building, or burn alive.

Now, you and I can see from our firmer emotional ground that there's no building and there's no fire. The activated nervous system of a person who lives with borderline isn't so clear-sighted. When combined with the impulsive urges detailed in the previous section, it's a little easier to see why the most horrific end is one so often realized by many of us who struggle with this condition.

My realest experiences with suicidal and non-suicidal self-harm began at fifteen and were all but over by twenty-one. Years removed from it, I can see it for what it was: an attempt to communicate something I didn't have the words for. No one in my life knew what was going on when it was actually going on. No therapist, family member, friend, or partner could've pried that out of me with the jaws of life. I couldn't have explained it, even if I tried to.

With no way to tell anyone exactly how bad things were, how suffocatingly smoky and hot those fires had gotten, I tried to show them. I was well-resourced enough to avoid the worst possible outcome. Many are not so lucky.

It's problematic to dismissively describe self-harming behavior as attention-seeking. Suicidality and non-suicidal self-injurious behavior are common symptoms of many mental illnesses and disorders (depression, bipolar, et cetera). Every person's experience with these "darker parts" of suffering is entirely unique. Understanding these is harm prevention, and they all must be taken seriously.

At the same time, there's an element of attention-seeking to *some* borderline self-harm. Each of us is always looking for a mechanism to express the level of pain we experience. Self-injury and suicidal behavior in people living with borderline is often an expression of the intensity of those negative emotions: *I am in so much pain. Please make it stop.*

Suicidality and self-harming behaviors are the end of a long biological and behavioral chain that escalates in tandem with emotional dysregulation, and ends with a desperate act. In almost all cases, borderline or not, suicide is an act of desperate expression, an exclamation that the emotional burdens of daily life are simply too much to tolerate.

Many people who have suicidal thoughts are terrified to share them due to the swath of consequences such an admission could bring their way: intense stigma, institutionalization, et cetera. The sooner we understand this, the sooner we can intervene and provide real, lasting support to address the many social, political, and psychological sufferings that lead people to this end.

Most of these poems were written when I was either actively self-harming in some form or were written about those experiences. They are among the oldest poems in this collection. From where I sit, many of them carry a more confessional undercurrent than the rest of my work. I would not write this way now. Even now, as I generally enjoy my life and have no desire for it to end, these poems remain deeply personal, bearing the markings of the most intimate struggles I've had with myself. I still feel a lot of shame and guilt around my experiences with suicidality – the fact that I'm here, and others aren't.[3] A few of them reflect on others' struggles.

These poems aren't particularly graphic or obscene, which speaks to the nature of some self-injurious and suicidal behaviors. There are sometimes no warning signs. Some of my longest nights weren't spent alone in my bedroom, or wandering aimlessly, or in hospital beds. Many of them were spent with other people, who were by and large unaware of the extent to which I was struggling. They saw no fire, smelled no smoke. They couldn't have.

Despite the challenges I've faced in my life, I've had a very rich existence. I have a loving family, exceptionally devoted friends, a beautiful place to call home, a stable career, and many talents at which I excel. Gratitude is not just about being thankful when things go your way. It's as much about being thankful when they don't. I have my scars and marks, as we all do. I'm profoundly lucky that I had access to the care that I did. It's our responsibility to make sure that everyone has access to the same level of care, too.

---

[3] This section is dedicated to my friend, C. We went to school together and stayed in touch intermittently over the years that followed. We weren't close, but it never felt that way. When I did what every politico-bro interested in politics does and started an ill-advised podcast in college, he listened to every episode. When things got scary for me, he came to the city with his partner. We met up briefly, and my brain was somewhere else, but I always appreciated him making that time for me. He sent me some of his poetry during COVID, and I loved it. A few weeks before he died, he called me to talk about what he was going through. Even though we weren't close, I got the sense that he felt safe confiding in me. We were supposed to see each other that year; we never did. He was an incredible person who even from a distance made a lasting mark on my life. He cared a lot about people. I think of him often.

Haze

Here I am, God, beneath miles of raw winter & it
builds towards a height, my breath smoking in the rays
             of fluorescent light here in this tundra.
Somewhere the answers are flashing themselves dizzy,
far enough to not touch, close enough to not see.   I
always thought I was tall enough, & yet as my psyche
is bounding at the walls of my downcast mind, I ask
a prayer – grow me taller. Let me hop the rooftops
in fiery stride, making haste to whisk those tomorrows
from the haze

Burning

Slow cook smell stinks of ash
palms   & frozen fingers
ashcans filing into the keys
as everything is   burning
kerosine fires   & stardust
wastebaskets   & jet fuel
here   & now
everything's burning –
just look at all of the smoke

August 17th

In the nightmare, you & I lie supine
    across from each other in a crypt
    below girded mounds of dirt;

You've not so much as said your name
        before your ether turns to honey,
golden mist rolling down your spectacles

I crave to know if your eyes still glow
        under the belly of the dusks,
        or if such things went with the rest of you

The Omni Parker House

A strange woman went cold today,

> Had her share of secrets
> Went into the morning
> Left them all unspoken

We sat at the library windows,
    watching them tarp the body,

Sat there at the grief spectacle,
cops & firemen circling the grave,
asking no one in particular,

What do we do now? & insight
told me to pray for a minute,
clear the shock from the deck,

hold vigil for someone who
            was someone, too.

Staring from Sodom to Aquarius

Let my words be canonized & my soul
    be marked rotten for salvation;

My words can travel the cosmic infinity
    at the speed of light, while my soul sits
    still on the edge of the delirious river,
    cupping the toxins from the water;

He wanted so badly to chase satellites
    towards the Moon, realizing only in time
    that the Moon was a lonely old man
    staring at Paris' nighttime yellow, consecrating
    the Godly metals floating between the planets
    until the next gnostic comes out of the womb
    & volleys him to the constellations

Contrition

God, they always told me not to ask questions,
       all of my thoughtful ones are scared secrets

I wash my hands six times a day & haven't gone to
confession since I started drinking whiskey

I beg for an end though it is selfish to ask

Standing here in this impossible quicksand, boneless,
          I am screaming contrition into the halos
        above the moaning city,

creaking beneath the weight of all of my sad prayers

Contemplating

There is no place for me here,
I bark up at the heavens

close my eyes & see petunias
coming up between the weeds

petunias & fine things,
petunias & worn silks

not these pills & this bottle of rot
the stuff that makes a man limp,

inglorious things so violent that I, too,
have become a strain of wretched

I languish through the unbelief
& am gifted only the wearing silence

of the predawn

The Night

The night, gnarling back at me
    as if we are engaged in this kind of epilogue,
    in which it expounds on the dusky points
    & says, *Alone, faithless, aren't you?*,

nothing left but the nighttime
to stare at & the nighttime does not blink,
        & so the look pieces itself together
          telling all I must know

Gallows Hunting, East Boston

On these stickiest nights, my English comes to rest
at the ear of the chickadees between the tenements,
& even here, in this place where so much has come
ablaze, there is an wide silence.   *Great one*,
something whispers, & I know now that these
series of questions are for the longtime to answer, not I,
not while caught in the maws of it, thrashing, limping
as I chuff shorts & let the fireballs of dead feeling
take hits at me slowly. I know on these nights,
long nights, cruelest nights, my words mean nothing
to the deafest ears & that I am but a cantor
for the absence of light, just screaming
on another of these nights

Belmont '19

I seek you in the rain,

between cracks of lightning,
 through these deep puddles

This is not the time for these questions,
            & yet I ask them to the moon

She is like you.
She knows everything.

After Pablo Neruda (1904-1973)

Manchester Holiday Inn Express

I am sulking in a loveless motel king bed
as bassheads play with needles through the wall

I will shoot out the lights & cover my head
with shell casings to allow myself a closeness with it,

an unresolving whiteout evening alone,
swimming lost inside this wettest nightmare

Man on the Uptown 1 Train

Man holds a finger gun to his temple
  & pulls the finger trigger,
    shaking his wallet by his ear,
    listening for free change
  from Chambers to Fourteenth,
  rattling his way along as cruel November
  comes to expiration, beneath acid city,
  roaring along – the traincar slips
  & the man goes sailing into the seats,
  change curling into the lap of a woman
  who takes it penny by penny, as if
  to count it, returning it to the man
  in handfuls like sipping water,
  & they exchange this somber look,
  a human kind of wanting,
  as the train punches through Chelsea
  & all is made a sideways cast of right

Death Wish

My blood is thicker than midwinter sea foam
            is dying to drive itself insane

& I am the afterthought in this, tangled in myself,
     am not too much for the taking

I know the doleful desire for it, the new
   form of wanting, until I catch your eyes –

       As time slows to a stop, we see each other
           & I say,

Take it from me, now. Carry it along & I will meet you
in a place we can plop it down together, let it fill the forest,

leave it alone for its own benign end.

Oceans Away

I space myself out at the churning Atlantic,
  thinking my way back into it, that long night

I heard word & the world became shapeless,
               tasted sort of a glass of bitters

If I was stronger than I was,
  I would have hauled you up with me
  pumped the water out of your lungs

Prating on about H.W., the new war,
  monstrous Kissinger & lo fidelity acid rock
  whirring around us on the old farm,

heavens only know the possibilities
but I imagine & smile through rivers,

taking from the edge of grief

for C (1996-2021)

6. Affective instability due to a marked reactivity of mood (e.g., intense episodic dysphoria, irritability, or anxiety usually lasting a few hours and only rarely more than a few days).

I'VE TAKEN TO DESCRIBING life with borderline as living with an emotional switch when everyone else has a dial. From the earliest stages of my childhood, I've always been a remarkably emotional person. Hearing the stories my mother has shared about the things I did, the way I interacted with the world, clued me in on the origins of my condition. It bears repeating: borderline is as much a physiological condition as a psychological one. Once you understand this, a host of borderline-induced behavioral patterns make a little more sense.

I recognized early on that boys and men were not supposed to have feelings. I've found through my friendships and relationships with women that this social norm was almost entirely constructed by men, even if it's sometimes reinforced by others. It's a damaging expectation, and contributes to so much of the pain that podcast con-artists and strongmen and Internet potion peddlers have foisted upon us as a collective over the past decade. In that way, I suppose I was blessed to have developed a personality disorder. I couldn't *not* feel, even if I tried.

Women make up the vast majority of patients diagnosed with borderline. For every three women diagnosed with the condition, one man receives the same diagnosis[1], despite the scientific consensus that the condition is equally prevalent in both men and women[2]. As a culture, we've come to associate emotionality with femininity, as if feeling things has a gender. Gender norms extend to every aspect of Western life, including psychiatry. None of this is shocking or profound if you think about it even a little bit.

Affective instability is the core defining feature of borderline. No other neurosis or symptom described in this collection runs through the rest with the same consistency. It's very common for the intensity of borderline to be mistaken for something else. One study suggests as many as 40% of people living with borderline are misdiagnosed as bipolar II[3], just as I was.

In fairness to the field of psychology, there's substantial overlap between borderline personality and bipolar disorders, specifically within the context of this criterion. Dual diagnoses are not uncommon, and the symptomatic schema overlaps heavily. There are, however, subtle differences in the emotional functioning of the bipolar and borderline brains. My moods will shift over the course of a day, whereas your average person with bipolar disorder experiences the same over the course of weeks or months.

---

[1] Kristalyn Salters-Pedneault. (2020, November 25). *Borderline Personality Disorder Statistics*. Verywell Mind; Verywellmind. https://www.verywellmind.com/borderline-personality-disorder-statistics-425481

[2] Sansone, R. A., & Sansone, L. A. (2011). Gender patterns in borderline personality disorder. Innovations in clinical neuroscience, 8(5), 16-20.

[3] Ruggero, C. J., Zimmerman, M., Chelminski, I., & Young, D. (2010). Borderline personality disorder and the misdiagnosis of bipolar disorder. *Journal of psychiatric research,* 44(6), 405-408. https://doi.org/10.1016/j.jpsychires.2009.09.011

The rapidly shifting nature of my emotional experience can be disorienting. The emotional static is nearly constant. Meditation has always been a difficult practice. Silence and stillness are still a little elusive. I consider the few moments I have them extremely sacrosanct.

Dealing with the emotional intensity I experience every day requires me to do something very foreign: ignore the impulse to act on my feelings. I feel a million things a minute, and those million things cause a million thoughts, which prompt a desire to act in ways that *feel* completely rational but are actually a little bit totally nuts. You simply can't trust your brain when your brain is actively being poisoned by the intensity of your feelings.

My understanding of my feelings has evolved over the past few years. I recognize now that I lived much of my life hoping to either change them, ignore them, or suffocate them. I judged the size of them, too. This is not a helpful way of living with borderline. It's true that my condition causes me to experience things more intensely, and denying that does nothing but repeatedly invalidate my way of existing in the world. More generally, denying and repressing your feelings isn't a healthy way of living, period.

Feelings are seen as a kitschy thing, the concern of poets and shrinks and diaries. They're a far more important part of human experience than we readily admit. Emotion regulation is not just a means of coping with conditions such as borderline; it's harm prevention, social intervention, and political praxis. Think of how many wars and crimes and war crimes could be prevented if the instigators of such things merely took the time to stop and self-regulate? What if we made emotion regulation a core part of public school curricula? What if we integrated such lessons into our judicial system in lieu of the current carceral mess? I could write a book on that, too.

Before I took my condition more seriously, my rational acuity contrasted sharply with my emotional functioning. I had the intellect of a well-read adult, and baseline emotion regulation skills of a toddler or teenager (depending on the hour or day). The things that set me off were so banal that I often refused to believe they were the true cause of my distress. I have a tendency to get stuck in my own brain, to attempt to think my way out of emotional dysfunction and assign deeper meaning to emotions that are provoked often by very small things, or sometimes nothing at all. I intellectualize my feelings, and it does me no favors. The simple truth is that what others feel as a pin prick feels to me like a harsh blow to the gut. It's my responsibility to deal with that appropriately.

Radical acceptance of the reality of my feelings allowed me to start the long, arduous process of managing them. There are often many vacillating feelings and thoughts bouncing around my brain. They often don't mean much of anything. I first had to accept them, their size, and the ways in which they impacted my view of the world before I could do anything else. I interrogate my own emotions, asking questions of circumstance and fact. It's an odd process, but one that works quite well. Much of the time, the answer is simple: it's because I have a complex personality disorder.

Feelings are a funny thing. They both function as a part of our lived reality and an influencing factor on how we perceive it. People who live with borderline have such intense emotional experiences that our momentary emotions often exercise an undue influence on our perceptions of the world (see Criterion 9). We all have feelings, and we all have moments in which those feelings put pressure on our thoughts and behaviors. Borderline merely ratchets that pressure up by an order of magnitude.

118

102nd Floor, Empire State Building

I am fifteen & my mother & I
are looking out at steaming Jamaica

& the elevator attendant looks at me,
says in a nighttime gentle voice,

There is no place in the world
                    like New York City

Hopping mad city of food truck cab fare,
   air heavy with tire marks & trash-stink

Endless miles of open storefront neon sign
   cluster storm dream traffic light chirping,

neophyte loud-mouthed beauty queens
   hanging bedsheets out of windows

   waving white flags of surrender, as if to say,
   Okay, alright, you win, New York

June

oh wow
oh wow
the sky pale
dew-drop clear, & a
  series of ropes build to a
sennit chain in my stomach
shackled to the walls
hanging around
through all of
June

Stinkboats

How wonderful!
The sight of a million
    floating stinkboats
rowing in the currents
smallest leaves, fry-cooked
browned, tarred, lifting,
dragging beside the shore
a million stinkboats
clean and endless

Autumn '16

'16, autumn, president's gone & my worries
  are pyramids in a field of wheat

If each refrain were different, the songs
  would be brilliant

                    Instead, monotone
                    Instead, delirious

If God is dead & man can *What if?* himself
  into oblivion, I will soon become a nothing

I will peel back my layers
I will break bread with sinners

My insecurities are flurries in this machine,
    each different, each an aubade for the gone world

The snowstorm breaks & the city is murky quiet,
    & if I am alone I am lost about it, blessedly naive

November Blues

Longest month is so short.
Bites at my new perception of time.
I watch as the men in Moscow hats run
towards the train platforms, look towards the sky
& watch the weighty day collapse,
wrap itself down to a cooling evening.
Time angrily tearing page to page on the wall,
so much of it simply gone, we can't get it back!
It's enough to give me the November blues.

Chelsea Nights

Newly winter & I am trekking down to it again
walking the coffeehouses on 23rd Street
as the river rumbles & dull autumn leans slow
down high rise New Jersey

Something is here, & the spectral things cough
in the thick street smoke, chanting the names
of the many dead until the morning light

Crossing Brooklyn Bridge

Biting cold morning, wind flicking
    off the banks of the East River

& I hike up the slope from City Hall
    to take the center & take pause

to gaze down at the shaky ebb,
    young flow, slowing at the pilings

below the thick February brick air
    sitting all over the place as a flagstone

pressing around on every skitter,
    us on the Bridge, taxicabs & pigeons,

fluttering all in sorry skyscraper winds
    planted in the groundswell of a feeling

I cannot name

Walk Home Between Torrents

Everything can be sacred if you dream it.
It rains like this & that as the corners
    swallow shoes, soaked to soles
the name in the sidewalk filling with water
the fetid suffering gargling out the leadpipe,
the empty room, the tumbling summer,
    suffering at a chance for difference,
    slackening the ropes in the machinery,
the rainstorms washing the chalk off
    a whole bellowing simile of blessings

If

If, then fireflies or a budding faith

If an unbeliever, reach out & touch,
    for once be bravest in the low want

If, then try, even if cratering out
    even if doubting tepid nervous,

If, then smile

Machine

I am on the edge of every circle in which I fit
        standing on the corner, waiting for sun
        to wash away the x's on my hands

The music pounds under the disco gaze,
        these dancers slide around, & certainly

I understand it now, everything is but temporary
    illusive, never to be seen or held
    only statuary in this stasis

    tension between bleeding reality & not
    pulling me apart away

Somehow

Somehow natural to lose ones mind,
                given to lose

Somehow staring at the hot furnace
as my underwear tumbles through
                cycles of dying

Thinking of those hauntings here beneath
the broken ceiling lamp,
All of my thoughts tangled in whites

Somehow nothing came of it
Somehow security
Somehow not

Communication by Impact

The brain is a freak-show convention on opium,
    a barking carnival of starlight on a beach,
    full of sun kissed conventionally attractive
        members of a class of artists,
through which a man with a bullhorn is always running,
        screaming about the end of the world,
& I am living in the middle of his forever news cycle,
          inside of my mind that is always telling me
  that the world is going to end at sundown
& that it is my last true chance at an honest thing
& truth is the slant rhyme that cuts through time
  so I will yell my truths, hurl them at a lonely bystander,
  throw the weight of the thing around
  while cutting it down to the static

March 21st

If you can, remember joy or the pennywort
　　at the muddy creeks,　　or maybe lilyponds
　　brined with living. The white pine, the
　　bracing nights
　　　　　　　　　In another world we've everything,
the gentle wind, the first look

In this world, we remind ourselves how
　　to pantomime surviving, a kind of fatalism,
the way the sun slat falls through the window,
& we remember it will soon be enough

7. Chronic feelings of emptiness.

THERE'S THIS ACHING FEELING that settles low in my center from time to time, a hollow little thing that I can point to but never explain. I know it when I feel it, even if I can't always verbalize it to myself or others. Chronic emptiness is the most difficult of all the diagnostic criteria to accurately portray. Even the scientific literature recognizes this. There are volumes upon volumes of research on borderline; few of them tackle this specific, persistent aspect of the condition.

Throughout my adolescence, I couldn't help but feel that there was a noticeable difference between my experience of my childhood and that of my friends. I had that recognition as it was happening, too, as did my various therapists and doctors. I was diagnosed with some form of depression during my sophomore year of high school, adding another label to the growing list of diagnoses in my medical records: generalized anxiety, ADHD, ODD, etc.

Clinicians will not diagnose a personality disorder in individuals under eighteen, under the working theory that 'personality' is highly elastic during adolescence. However, many parts of my experience of self – including an aching loneliness, an emptiness of sorts – remained. The poems in this collection span fifteen years of my life, all the way from sixth grade to my late twenties. It was all always there, somewhat the same. Borderline can mimic the symptomatology of each of my previous diagnoses. It brings with it the eccentricity of ADHD, the emptiness of depression, the chemical chaos of anxiety, the wide swings of bipolar disorder, and the rage of ODD. My symptoms were in plain sight for years. They were acknowledged, but wrongly attributed.

This loneliness and emptiness was not for a lack of company. I had lots of friends and lots of family. Without the words to describe what I was feeling, I began to suspect that there was something fundamentally wrong with me. In many ways, there was – that's not an uncommon feeling for people who experience childhood trauma. In the place where my self was supposed to be, there was an expansive void that became so normalized to my consciousness that I began to see it as a part of who I was. I began to feel alienated from my peers and eventually from myself.

In the context of my own struggle with my condition, chronic emptiness serves as both a form of avoidance of emotions and a kind of dissociation from myself. It's rarely a conscious state for me. It exists as an undertow to the rest of my experiences, a yearning beyond mere ennui. Like many feelings, boredom is a very intense experience for me. Depression is a condition strapped to chemical deficiencies and circumstances that, together, create a deep sense of hopelessness. Emptiness is a composite of intense boredom, disconnect, and apathy.

You'll find that each of these diagnostic criteria, including emptiness, shares many commonalities with the others. Several of the poems in this section could've been at home elsewhere. This is true for all the other criteria. There are poems which describe my experience of emptiness (see

'The Patina Method') that could easily describe issues with identity. There are others that were written about my attempts to cope with emptiness (see 'Dinner & a Film'). Descriptions of substance abuse as emotional numbing carry echoes of the works in the section on impulsivity and reckless behavior (see 'Fireside').

Understanding the way these symptoms play off each other is the result of a lengthy self-interrogation that I began to undertake as I pulled this collection together. Fear of abandonment (1) can lead to anxious, near-paranoiac rumination (9). Impulsivity (4) leads to suicidality (5). Fear of abandonment (1) and fear of engulfment (2) create a relational tension. Emotion dysregulation (6) can lead to extreme expressions of said emotions (8).

In my experience, a lack of identity (3) is the chief cause of the chronic emptiness I've felt throughout my life. The self exists entirely in one's own brain, and it anchors itself to the experiences of the body – to sensation. It's alarming to reach for the safety of shore and find yourself in the deadest zone of ocean. Without a firmly rooted sense of self, it's all too easy to float away.

Like all chronic health conditions, borderline is not a "fair" thing. Each of us is making our best efforts to fill a hole we didn't ask for, didn't create, and weren't properly taught how to manage. We're all trying to suture shut our own wound. This is a painful process. To extend the analogy: consider undergoing open-heart surgery while wide awake, listening to the shuffling and clanging of the operating room, feeling every pinch and nick. Sometimes, you just need to deal with it.

As I grew healthier, I found myself recognizing exactly how chronic emptiness impacted me as a child, adolescent, and young adult. I struggled to remain present in the better moments of my life. Being alone was very difficult (see Criterion 1), and it was in moments when I was alone that the floating void began to consume me. I drifted through much of my life, disconnected from the world and people around me. When I finally found something (or someone) to hold on to, I gripped it (or them) like a vice and refused to let go.

That void used to swallow everything that came its way. For years, I frantically tried to fill it with progressively more intense, self-destructive coping mechanisms: binge drinking, heavy drug use, intense relationships, et cetera. Even still, the void swirled, now carrying noxious detritus in its orbit, banging up against lots of other people as it spun. It was the monster that grew hungrier as it was fed.

I find that I've felt a little fuller since I began to develop myself and lean into the things I know that bring me joy. I began to starve the void and feed my soul. We all feel fuller when we're working to develop ourselves into something better, someone fuller. Understanding how to fill my own cup has been a challenge. It's required a lot of trial and error, and it's also been very fun. Finding a sense of purpose is a key part of living a human life – part of Ortega's grand project of being. It doesn't have to be a miserable, painful thing.

The many aspects of my personality that I've worked to develop have played a big role in my healing. I play guitar far more now than I did when I was at my worst. I've re-engaged with my childhood hobbies, such as building Lego sets and going on photography walks and arguing relentlessly about politics. I've discovered new, constructive activities that make me feel something intense but harmless. I make a more conscious effort to be present in moments that allow for connection and positive experience. There's been plenty of writing, too.

The Patina Method

There's an elephant in the room,
round gray-graphite thing, it is,

a long-winded old sketch,
hawking down at me off the wall,

& when the birds kick the light
in the bathroom & flutter about

I can't help but feel it; I'm in it
with the birds & the elephant

& I feel them in raptures; not inside
or out, a coat of varnish on them

or just dust

Dinner & A Film

That first winter here weighed a ton,
more than any of us could stand

                    Friend was sick
            & I was laughing in the streets,

play fighting with the Gods & O'*****
                    after a bottle of Christmas

He let us be & we felt the weight of
                our one last desperate act

as we began ravaging our way
to the empty stars

Hoboken, New Jersey

Hoboken is almost going gone, a den of thieves,
    as I attend to the cooking Hudson, chilling
    at the foot of the spritz of low autumn clouds,
    ash-stained jet stream streaking away,
    staring down Manhattan as the day snarls,
    hurling my name through the tuliptrees

Lamentation

So lost that I forgot how
    to find the hummingbirds buzz

Sweet wasted words whispered
    between glasses of claret

Now, alone with the wolves
      clamping down on the chaos,

        I howl along to the harvest moon
        smokesignaling for something lost

Manna

I walk down Maverick Street under stale dusk,
where it feels like the world is ending,

& a woman asks out of her front door,
Where is the bread?

        & a man stares at his feet & says,
I do not have it

Bake us some, here, tonight, she commands

Sometimes like his eyes I am as heavy
as an atom bomb or a satchel of God

I think for a moment about the soft violence
that enraptures us all,

how we live in an emotional sandstorm of our doings

In this stillness, I smell gasoline, light a match
& laugh as this world begins to smolder beneath my feet

So I bake us some bread & the sand pounds down
& she asks me,
       Where is the bread?

I open my palms for her and the Earth unfolds

I become the fortune teller, & I say,
        Allelujah, manna

Sundown

How do we patch up the sinkhole?

Just a child,   a ladybug,

as the carnival shut down behind him,
without reason, no resolution,

a birdsong or reckoning, just a tract of space
where a beating heart writhes live,

maybe forever, at least for now

Flight 831, Boston to LaGuardia

     Connecticut is a thicket of death,
&   Springfield is   obvious silent

Low fog shelf latches to stratosphere,
   snow strung across the riverbanks,

   Newburgh, amorphous foliage,
O how holy, untouched starved almost

Engine hum buzz over quiet February
   drowning the regular pedal of worry

Transmutations

No, not nothing, but not something either,
    just a riddle, short coarse & briny, sifting
    through my mouth as coffee & butterscotch
I will burn my name into the ground as it stales,
  in the stars & the space between them & we will
  call it fates, & when I die, they will plot roses at my feet,
      & I can establish myself in the many seasons,
    reject the protean temptations, see something
    with a permanence, a keeping beauty in me

Poem for Harlem

If you wish for something, will it & it shall be –
   the beggars lock arms & sing hymns
   in front of Saint Borromeo's, sucking on cans of PBR,
   hosting dreams of something different

Overpass creaks down the side streets of Columbia,
         CCNY & housing projects a mouse & the lion,
late-summer sun slouching around, kicking the tires,
sad caravans crawling towards Philly, the Potomac
& Port Elizabeth, winding westward all evening long

  Where do we go? The question scratches,
& so I say it to no one in particular, muse on it;
There is something here for me, certainly,
& I will find it sooner if I lose on looking

April, Counting the Dead

If there were such a thing as irony,
   these timings would not exist
    & the dead would ride alive with us

   There are only a few right times
         in this life

I used to be a true Catholic
  until the Universe rang the quailsong

Now, we count the dead each night,
      & pray to empty Heavens

that the Universe should be ironic, too

Church Street

Fleshy October, caught up in the size of things
   my hands, my baggage & my memories

I have always been caught up in the size of things

Church Street still as a bolt & on the bookshelves
  my alphabetized agonies work into neat rows,

& I am holding my tongue with my teeth
   as I run my fingers across the leathers

   searching for the one to give myself to wholly
   keep me preoccupied across the dirty season

Fireside

When I meet her, she is blackout drunk
& says that someone shot himself last year
   says she found him there,
     points up to a bedroom window

& I am silent, a church mouse or sheepish monk,
& I keep looking to you the way Christians pray
   as this burly drunken man falls towards me
   before he catches himself on my shoulder

We stand here & the burly drunken man sings
& I cannot help but intuit from this ordeal
   that there is a sad thing here,
     one husking quiet pile,

& that I was by myself but never alone

West Boylston, Massachusetts

I gaze out at Jupiter, the moon
& the lounging dog, cotton-mouthed

pulling smoke, watching smoke,
taking rough survey of the hedge line

sun crawling over a berm, coffee hot,
dewey quiet morning builds itself

from still nighttime, again, nothing
again, nothing, this dry cycle in want

Monday Morning

Monday coming on strong, now coalescing
below shelf clouds & a bluegray static wind
Up early spinning in it, wanting at something new,
a day unmade & making always.
Sprouting up outside the vestiges of a wind,
a looking, intuition to thunderheads.
The eggs turning slow in the pan, cracking out
across the kitchen, a gentle sizzling, & so I ask no one
in particular, *How would you like your eggs?*
& recall that I get to decide about the eggs,
the Monday, the day unmade, my own curiosity
carrying a sense of duty.
I will fry the eggs, degrease the cast iron.
I will build the day from its parts to a whole.

8. Inappropriate, intense anger or difficulty controlling anger.

BORDERLINE RAGE IS A FOUL THING, an all-consuming and regularly terrifying form of destruction. I'm intimately familiar with its corners and expressions. Even so, it doesn't run as deeply through my writing as the other diagnostic criteria. When I experience intense anger, I can do little else but work with it and do my best to keep it tame. I have no time to wax poetic on it.

I was a poorly-behaved child, prone to outbursts, tantrums, and frequent disrespect of authority. For my first decade, I spent more time in the principal's office or the hallway outside the classroom than I did learning. For one reason or another, I was always doing something to piss someone off. Anger came easily to me. "Most of Nicholas' emotions are expressed as anger," my early medical records read. The focus of any corrective treatment in those early years was on reducing aggression and anger; the other emotions and experiences, many of which were not visible, were secondary considerations.

My anger was in part a socialized behavior. I grew up in a volatile household, where displays of intense anger were commonplace. Even if physical violence wasn't enacted against another person – no one was beaten in my home – proximity to that level of anger and dysfunction left a mark. I noticed the free-floating anger in my body long before my diagnosis. It pointed itself everywhere, but nowhere more sharply than at my family and closest friends.

Anger is the one affective expression that our culture universally allows men to entertain without judgement. We're socialized from a young age that anger is *the* acceptable expression of the male emotional experience. At this moment in our history, we're seeing the terrible results of that implicit rule; the whole show is run by the angriest, smallest people you could possibly imagine. No crying, smiling, giggling, frolicking. Yelling, however, is perfectly fine. For many men – myself included – anger is often an expression of something else, something that we're taught to keep out of view.

In the context of borderline, some theorize that the anger itself is not the issue, but rather the affective expression of the emotion that makes it a clinical feature of the condition. So-called "anger rumination" – defined as "repetitive thinking about anger experiences and the causes and consequences of angry feelings" – is a contributing factor to the explosive displays of anger associated with borderline rage[1]. As with most emotions, the core of the dysfunction is not so much the emotion itself, but how we manage (or fail to manage) it.

As with all emotions, anger is often an all-or-nothing thing to the borderline mind. I am almost never a *little* angry. I may be very angry for a little *while*, and still, the amplitude

---

[1] Oliva, A., Ferracini, S. M., Amoia, R., Giardinieri, G., Moltrasio, C., Brambilla, P., & Delvecchio, G. (2023). The association between anger rumination and emotional dysregulation in borderline personality disorder: A Review. *Journal of Affective Disorders, 338,* 546-553. https://doi.org/10.1016/j.jad.2023.06.036

of the anger remains disproportionately vast. Triggers include perceived abandonment, difficult interpersonal situations, feeling betrayed, persistent stress, and emotion dysregulation.

As I began to explore the lasting impacts that different childhood traumas had on my life, I found myself getting even angrier. I carried a lot of raw anger for a long time. I was angry at the world for the ways in which it failed to protect me as a child. I was angry at myself, which is in part why that person is the one who I always wanted to destroy. I was also angry at anyone who tried to love me, because I couldn't fathom that anything about me was truly worthy of love. I existed as a wolf in a foot trap: screaming for help, and then trying to rip off the arms of whoever came to free me.

For a while, I was totally unaware of where that anger came from – it was a fire with no clear cause that burned its way right through my being. When I realized its origins, I was no longer angry – just desperately sad.

I knew I had to find an outlet for this ugly thing outside of processing it in a clinical setting. Anger can be a heavy emotion to carry, and it wears us down. Physical exertion has been a boon for my emotion regulation skills. I often power walk miles at a time. I bought a Peloton, and recently began going to the gym a few days a week. It sounds almost caveman-ish, but throwing around heavy things does incredible things for the soul. Exerting emotional energy focusing on physical sensation is a very effective way at managing emotions, particularly negative ones.

Righteous anger, of course, is never wrong – only wrongly expressed. I've always been enraptured by politics. I had a sense from an early age that something rotten was going on in our body politic, but could never pin it down. I felt that I was destined to become a lawyer or a politician. That didn't really work out because it clashed with my desire to be a better person, and I didn't want to be angry all the time. To this day, I find myself getting increasingly angry as I write about national affairs. I write far less about politics than I used to for that very reason – not because I don't care, but because I care too intensely for it to be a healthy thing if done regularly. I save my words for the most important things.

Anger is not always a bad thing. Sometimes, it's an expression of courage. Being angry at the state of things when the state of things is so bleak is an appropriate emotional response. These are very difficult times for even the most put-together people. The brutality of modern life has never been so plainly set before the masses. If you open your phone at the right moment, there's a good chance that you'll see something that provokes irascible anger before you even leave bed.

Like all emotions, anger serves a purpose. It can motivate us to make changes, say the things we need to say, and remove ourselves from harmful situations. There are good fights to fight. We all must fight them. Channeling our anger into the right things is a healthy habit we all ought to build into our own lives more consistently.

A lot of my prevention work has centered around keeping things more level. Age and maturity have helped. Accepting the anger I carry and directing it into productive activities – including writing – has made it far easier to manage. The work was always finding ways to make the anger appropriate in its velocity and in its expression. This is meaningful work; the world could do with a lot less free-floating, inappropriate anger.

Holy ****!

it's obscene
a bad gesture
foul-mouthed thing
curling in the wind;
a straight line, no frills,
monologue on Dante,
a dog in heat
holy
holy

Bastard

The place is always riddled with questions –
  the dead neighbor, the soldiers, & that old bastard

& I, dangling my legs off the low-roof, rinsing my insides,
   staring out at an infinite night, a messing thing,

spotlighting for his marble eyes, long gone in it,
  howling at God & foaming sharp at the mouth like a dog,

swearing off the drinker in me, that sort of madness,
  watching the Perseids rain down as time blows it open,

his radioactive soul & drops of holy water,
my mother's tears, dripping into the Earth,

washing the streets clear with answers

Personality

Shaking is mood rising, sun-starved flower,
as if spring were an animal rattling at its cage

My hiding thing came animate, sobbing
at the enormity of the decaying wound

Rather   only whispers in meter,
never quiet enough for me to hear them,
seeping through into the longer things
we say

Borderline

The blender full of glass sharpens itself.
    In another life it shines on & forward,
    in this I am maybe roaring at the sun,
                maybe staring at the skyline,
asking questions, never finding answers,
because it's bad luck, could blow 'em up.

Imagine it – a world with no stars
& the nights just a pale loneliness.

Need not imagine, paint that picture.

Anniversaries

What do we say on these grey days?

All of the worst words have left me speechless
They move slowly under a boulder of dulling joints

If there is a lesson in all of this, it is that no thing
is too small to be sacred to you & nothing is at all

Hymn

In the end there will be us –
there will be pining & feist &
drunkenness beneath those
purple mountains & hysteria
above the fruited plain as we
march lock-step towards the
divine chanting *The sun will
surely rise, it will, it will*
In the end there will be us –
in the dark the light goes bright

Washington, D.C.
January 21, 2017

160

Machiavelli

...was a nobody kingmaker but never a king,
     a snapping stray skulking around the nights

& so I sit on the veranda, sky behind Wompatuck
     turning long orange, think of the the long nights
     on which his soul burned from the fire,

Think of the grinding knife sinking deeper
    towards a fragile heart, leaking out secrets,
& I think to myself of Machiavelli,
  of the way his arms twisted in the strappado

  & the naked treachery that started & ended him,
of how the power was temporary,
of his insecurity, smallness, dead consideration
    spark hollow through time

Weeding in the Late Afternoon

May is cording itself up & I'm weeding between
the bushes in a yard that isn't mine.   There are
curfews in Denver & a dead boy in Detroit.   I
try to forget these things & twist out the chickweed,
but it weighs something on my amplifying conscience.
What are we for if not each other?   We haven't
dropped to a bottom, but we do float close to it.   I
hear 'em holler all day and night, tossing, disrupting
narrative space.   Gas is cheap & cowardice is cheaper.
A pathetic thing, a losing thing, power as intoxicant
as retributive finding. I pull my weeds, I pull my dirt –
gets beneath my fingernails, stuck in there – & I toss them
into the road to maybe plant some small flowers

Akeldama

The ghosts made it out down the back.
I see you wasting in between the warping beams,
cold-faced, rocking into it, lost in your finite Catholic hell,
lurching down at my infrangible corpus.
You buried me a thousand times, expectant, reckless,
choosing to yourself that I would stay the part,
ring-fought pit bull, coy & caught up in the world
you ranked for us, wasting & writhing
Looking back at that child I see nothing
but his softest being, unbitten resolve,
solid as the working tree, the multitudes of hoping
that you did not get on with, things unvitiated, venerated,
the things a man wants to hold tight in his memory,
& as I lock that door again I see him crack smile as to say,
I am here! I am here!

9. Transient, stress-related paranoid ideation or severe dissociative symptoms.

FOR A VERY LONG TIME, I believed wholeheartedly that there was no psychotic element to my condition. I was grateful for it. No one wants to believe they're capable of losing it; we're all, to ourselves, the most rational beings. I was always out there, maybe, but never quite psychotic.

Borderline makes handling emotional stress challenging. Under intense stress, the daily pressures of the condition can give way to a type of paranoia. This paranoia is markedly different from the psychotic paranoia present in patients diagnosed with schizophrenia and similar affective disorders. As with most emotional states, paranoia is a transient thing for people living with borderline; it's as quick to come as it is to go. So-called "delusions" are more emotional than sensory in nature; instead of "seeing things," people with borderline "feel things."

I've found that stress-related paranoid ideation is typically brought on by a failure to self-regulate to a sufficient extent that one's nervous system can give way to reason. I lived with chronic and untreated sleep issues for much of my adolescence and young adulthood, and I've noticed that a persistent lack of quality sleep is a major contributing factor to my developing such ideation. Prolonged periods of isolation and rumination are often warning signs of coming trouble.

When I arrive at a place of "paranoia", it never feels like paranoia. For a while, it felt wholly real, and no amount of reassurance was sufficient to clip it. I tend to hyper-fixate on solving so-called "impossible problems." Mine tend to center around betrayal, persecution, and loss of control. These problems are never fixable; that's in part by cognitive design. They allow for extensive rumination, but never resolution.

These "impossible problems" are closely linked to affective expressions of borderline: fear of abandonment, insecurity, chronic shame and guilt, or fear of the unknown. These could be about anything – mistakes, bad decisions, important relationships, the judgement of others, negative interpersonal experiences, et cetera – but they almost always involve a circular reasoning that would push anyone to their outer limits.

People who live with borderline are overrepresented in inpatient psychiatric settings. Somewhere around 1.4 percent of the general population lives with borderline[1], and yet it's estimated that people with borderline make up 20% of the inpatient population[2]. I suspect that two of the diagnostic criteria in particular – recurrent suicidal behavior and stress-related paranoid ideation – are driving factors behind involuntary hospitalization, and the general

[1] Lenzenweger MF, Lane MC, Loranger AW, Kessler RC. DSM-IV personality disorders in the National Comorbidity Survey Replication. *Biol Psychiatry*. 2007 Sep 15;62(6):553-64

[2] Biskin R. S. (2015). The Lifetime Course of Borderline Personality Disorder. *Canadian journal of psychiatry*. Revue canadienne de psychiatrie, 60(7), 303-308. https://doi.org/10.1177/070674371506000702

overrepresentation of people living with borderline in psychiatric healthcare facilities.

I learned in the most unfortunate way that, absent context, presenting to an outpatient provider with complaints of paranoia and a pattern of self-harming behaviors does not end well. I've got the socks to prove it. Each was a small traumatic experience in its own right. I don't talk about it often nowadays. It's not light cocktail hour conversation, and carries an impenetrable stigma of its own. I reached a point where I would've rather pretended it didn't happen.

It did happen, though, and I feel it's important to acknowledge that it happened. I didn't go through all of that for nothing. Besides, the place was always full, so it wasn't just me who went through it. My experiences with inpatient treatment weren't that miserable, but they were definitely unnerving. Again, I have a tendency to obsess over controlling outcomes – an itch that's impossible to scratch when a team of strangers are dictating your diet, routine, and movement for days at a time. I learned a lot about myself, as one does when they have little else to do.

Over the course of my treatment, I spent a good amount of time around people who were failed by the support systems many of us take for granted, or hardly think about outside of a news-making tragedy. I saw up close the impact socioeconomic factors can have on mental health, and how the gaping holes in our healthcare system exacerbate inequalities in outcomes. Money speaks every language.

The first place I ended up for treatment at fifteen was a very diverse unit. For the first time in my young life, I was in a situation where I, a white guy, was in the minority. I went to private school in one of the wealthiest parts of the country. My first experience with inpatient treatment was when I began to somewhat understand that we're all created equal, but some of us are treated more equally than others. I got out of there and went home to a loving family, and a system set up to ensure my success. Many of my peers had nowhere and no one to go home to.

There is widespread disagreement about the usefulness of the word "borderline" as a diagnostic label due to its initial meaning. The term "borderline" was intended to designate the place where the condition was believed to exist on the broad spectrum between neurosis and psychosis: right in the middle, see-sawing between. I understand the hesitation to stick with the label; it's stigmatizing, reductionist, and ignores the impact of lived experience.

I do feel like it's at least a little accurate, though, to say that borderline can cause emotional reactions so expansive and intense that they'd at least appear to many well-thinking, well-meaning people to be a form of semi-psychosis. There is a kind of reason to borderline paranoia and dissociation, even if it's the most unreasonable thing. The reason of the emotion-mind is forever warped by feelings. I certainly don't believe myself or anyone else with this condition to be psychotic – clinically or otherwise – but I do think we can appear it.

I discussed my experiences at length as they happened, and then not again for a long time. Even within the context of a stigmatized mental health condition, the idea of "losing one's own mind" – real, clinical psychosis – is taboo. But six years removed from the last of my inpatient treatments, I recognize the importance of being honest about my experiences with the most complicating aspect of any major mental health condition: the impact it has on how one perceives and experiences reality, and where that can lead. I'm beyond grateful that I had access to the best treatment in the world to bring me back to a safer reality. I think often about those who didn't.

Bengal Tiger

A bengal tiger lives in my closet

She has moss eyes & emerald pupils
& howls towards the hill where her lover

lay in wait, staring out of the keyhole,
waiting for the moon

The Existentialist's Bible

The word is bloodied
& I am an empty satchel of Christ,
as conscious as a wall lamp
                    that bedspread
Foresting on a Sunday evening
through a haunted house, where
            the snakes are closing in
        & the hourglass is dripping
faster by the minute, as the world
is turning faster on its heels
consuming my everything

Sylvia

Sylvia walks around the old block
with a worry on her face, drinking in
what is left of this stale Sunday. I watch her
go, leaning on the windowsill towards
the street, imagining. She saunters to the end
& back, repeating a race she never wins,
abstracting something like mimicking
a forgone conclusion.

This dialog continues for hours,
well beyond darkening, & I sit transfixed,
watching this walk as she begins to mumble,
then scream for not one of us to hear,
huddles with the rusting mailbox
& she looks up to see me, smiles,
begins her walk home.

Howl '17

I.

I saw the greatest minds of my generation
  destroyed by madness, screaming at their telephones,
               hysterical & high,

Selling themselves to the politicians,
       looking for someone to blame, finding no one
     & blaming the world, burning for revolution,

Who were nearly expelled from Catholic school
       by Hypocrites or shouting heresies of love & freedom
       as they flipped over tables in the Chapel,

Who made the lonesome Pilgrimage to Boston,
       smoking dreams away, read philosophy,
       went mad & stood on the steps of the state Capitol
       hollering canticles at the Night,

Who rioted in the November streets, screaming
       about fascists, returning home only to find
       Mother & Father sketching Mohammed on
       their doors in blood,

Who distributed Communist propaganda in the parks,
       weeping while the sirens of police cars
       wailed them down, & wailed down West,
       & the Green Line below also wailed,

Who watched drunks dance for change outside coffeeshops
       as businessmen mannequins laughed under the glow
       of baseball city & the full moon roared,
       the stadium roared & their loins roared, too,

Who slinked through Hoboken high to rancid dormitories,

Where they listened to the Hudson crack over rocks,
   pleading with Night to end the age-long poker game
   of War & Peace,

Who keeled over onto skyscraper foundations in Midtown
   before the long ride to Brooklyn, where they emerged
   from the tubes lost until the hotel crawled out
   of the pitch a block away,

Who were left for dead by their own false Prophets,
   awoke to Manhattan, picked themselves up
   out of hotel beds hung over with heartbreak
   & memory pain pulsing through their corpse,

Who journeyed to Boston, who died in Boston,
   who came back to Boston & waited in vain,
   who watched over Boston & brooded & loned
   in Boston until the city finally fell open at them,

Who packed ephemera & alcohol into boxes
   & trekked to the Island, where joyriding through
   the floodlights of Newport they searched for answers,
   finding only more questions,

Who returned home & nearly got busted in their trucks
   as they drove through New Bedford with two
   Barilla jars of greens, barely lifting a finger
   off the wheel the whole way there,

Who stabbed at their wrists three times unsuccessfully,
   were forced to bare their insides
   to pairs of eyes with PHDs who said
   they were going mad with sadness,

Who sulked in hospital beds in brown scrubs for Eternity,
   listening to schizophrenics hurl curses
   through the walls

waiting for the sweet salvation
of Death or discharge,

Who went grey & plunged into the concrete Void
    of Concerta, lithium & antipsychotics,
    pharmaceutical alphabet soup, all the way to Zoloft,
    THC & amnesia, tobacco & vodka dreams,

Who stood stunned silent in brick black Night shaking,
    Their naked soul held together
    by duct tape & drugs,

Who stood calling into the Void for answers,
    hearing in response
    only the howling echo of Time.

II.

ah, City, you have driven us millions mad,
    all of us who now cry out Day & Night,

Who are truly mad & got chained up in that place
    where they remain chanting,
    refusing medication, going on
    about the Rapture,
    doing everything in pairs to forestall it
    for just a short while longer,

Who shipped off to Hartford to study the mind
    & instead dropped acid, mainlined
    & gave themselves Mania, or a heart condition,
    then took their beauty Upstate
    & from there came home,

Who said the Kaddish & took pills
    & still saw Mother looming large,
    alive again waiting to take them in Her arms,

a dream from the Reagan era
which still haunts their sleep,

Who devoted themselves to Daughter
only to find Daughter dead from the neck up
frying in Sunlight, avoiding windows
& insisting the cancer would kill her
though the doctors knew otherwise,

Who, gone too soon, now stares back from the Void
informing opinions with Divinity,
not Scripture but Apocrypha acid
& a faucet of Bordeaux leaking
slowly from their eyes,

Who began to go mad in all of this,
knowing for seconds that they, too,
would one day see Mother & shake
at Her image & so told themselves
it was all just anxiety or hallucination,

Who thought they had lost their conscience
in the soup of otherness but were the same
as the next, not Prophets, & so cried
into notebooks for the Eternity to come,

ah, City, even the sane ones went mad
in your Night, all of them

Who slouched towards the sinking Sun,
wandering through minefields
listening to the subway cough up turpentine
into the air, vanishing for weeks at a time
to cast spells & whisper about intimacy, serenity
& other taboos,

Who grew lonesome in the West, made the Pilgrimage

east & buried the past with sex
& psychoactives, booze & Boy,
following the brilliant no-name
off the cliffs of insanity,

Who detested their reflection before the Pilgrimage,
Were swallowed whole by the Pilgrimage,
laid root in the City & spiked the watering hole
with our favorite flavor of Life,

Who became the middleman for them all who suffered,
went mad like the rest & grew resentful
of urban living, thinking only of the oasis
as they crawled thirsty through the sewer pipe
of emotional damage,

Who were frozen in Time
as the Madness of the western way came to them,
wished only to protect the others
from the Madness, lost the battle
& came out deadened, cold
& shaking to the core,

Who built funeral pyres in Mendon & drove
through some five hundred towns,
saw the Archangel of Souls
picking apart their memory
as the rain & snow covered the roads
for a million miles of night,

Who vodka drunk on Thursdays sowed happiness
In stuffy apartments, lighting cigarettes
on the walk home with radiant coolness
that could stifle the fires, raging on their shore
'till death parts the sea

Who died a hundred thousand times, high & hopeless,

alonesome, praying for deliverance or death
as the sound of love & joy hit the wall

III.

Kat – I'm with you in Providence,
        where your condition is reported as grave
        & graying, whole body drained of brilliance;

I'm with you in Providence,
    where you're sadder than I am,
    hiding in Night in blanket & nightgown,
    wandering the concrete halls;

I'm with you in Providence,
    where you must feel very strange & alone
    without them all who abandoned you there to die;

I'm with you in Providence,
    where we imitated the shade of our past,
    recounting the Passion with grand accuracy;

I'm with you in Providence,
    where we laughed at this invisible humor,
    at nurses who cracked jokes as souls cracked;

I'm with you in Providence,
    where we would make great lovers in another life,
    drinking from the bosoms of asylum dwellers;

I'm with you in Providence,
    Where you wept over the bodies of your step sisters
    as we screamed in a straightjacket that we were holy;

I'm with you in Providence,
    where you bang on the bathroom door screaming
    all hours accusing doctors of malpractice gran mal;

I'm with you in Providence,
 where we split the heavens above Rhode Island
 singing Hallelujah with our thirty mad comrades;

I'm with you in Providence,
 where you wake up drugged out of the coma
 into Womb & so choose to make like an airplane;

I'm with you in Providence,
 where in my dreams you wander
 on the highway across America in tears

to the door of my dormitory in the West Street night.

For K.G. and the CHIP children

After "Howl"
by Allen Ginsberg (1926-1997)

Walking Campus

The beauty factor of this day does not stiff the pain
          does complement it, greens & oranges
There is something to this freakish quiet
The world has nothing satisfying to say to us all
The hush of leaves flipping down the drive,
the hurling sweep winds, backfire of distant engines,
& as we walk by Bowditch, Oaks, deMarneffe,
the shrubs are shagging off the week-old autumn
I haven't felt this in some time, & the sickest ones
will not sense for more.
Suffering is a snarling thing of many shades,
mine still fairly routine as I am not gone into it
& there is a suffering still, a missing & waiting,
a yearning for a nominal stillness that remains clouded,
glory-brimmed thing on a weekend morning,
in a transubstantiated extraordinary place

Illness

I am the dog before thunder

Even with the comforter
    above my nose,

The shadow of the crucifix
        in the streetlight
        bright like day

If we were older,
we'd have done a different thing

& we were not so this is the thing,
        this loathly thing.

Antiphon

As the conspiracies grow louder
I am able to muster a simple prayer,

Something small but mighty,
so I say to no one,

Assure me that I am human.
Translate my gospel to knowing.

Hold my hand through miry night.
Allow me to remain patient, kind.

Daydreaming Up Impossible Situations

I go down to Chinatown in the rain,
& stint through lights from the storefronts,

dodging National Grid sewerpipe puffing
into cat cavernous wine dream bedtime;

My neuroses bloat to twice the size
that my hands could hold,

& there is a man with shotguns for an arms
officiating a wedding on the roof of the bus!

Midnight summer rain, bless me in these things,
Keep me full moons, keep me restaurant,

keep me,   moons, keep me.

Hay gente aun que te aman

You're sleeping soundly &
I roll over towards you & ask,

*What do you see when
you close your eyes?*

& you say nothing, chest
beating, mouth hanging,

Hay gente aun que te aman

& so I whisper it again,

*What do you see when
you close your eyes?*

& hear no answer
& I tease it against your neck,

*There are people here
who still love you.*

Cause Proximate

You do not have the knowing of me now
of the weighty sense that builds in my gut,
the cringing yen or all of the ghosts,
the way the want accretes or the way it is torn to pieces
or even the fleeting little things I have locked
in a corner of my heart; if it breaks, so be it,
let it fly out into some space I have created somewhere
above the suburbs of Denver, where I dropped a thing
from an airplane, told it to wait as I could foresee
its usefulness & now I feel this ominous sore metastasizing,
cropping up in our bedflow or in other exercise
of romantic living, such as the way I think people look
at me more than they ought to.
It is never what it is, never what it ought to be, just feeling,
cooling off inside castaway areas in my mind

Afterword and Acknowledgements

I'M SITTING OUTSIDE ON THE PATIO of a familiar, quaint café in a busy corner of Back Bay on what is both the last summer and first autumn day: seventies, spotty clouds, the trees beginning to hint at their first changing. I'm doing that thing I do where I hold onto the writing as long as I possibly can to avoid being vulnerable. I'm finding myself worried about saying exactly the right thing. I'm trying too hard to build the perfect narrative, so I step away from the work for a moment to think less on it.

Right up to the bitter end, I remained nervous about how this would go over. I worked hard to ensure that this collection didn't become an exercise in exhibitionism. Some things really ought to remain private. For as vulnerable as I've been here, there are many experiences that I still hold closer to my chest. Besides – suffering as art is a little cringy. I never suffered for the sake of art, even if many of the things I've created were born from suffering. I live my life as it happens, and document my experiences in my work. My art comes from the conditions in my soul, not from the experiences it describes.

I was hesitant to publish this for a lot of reasons. Many of the experiences and perspectives described in this

185

collection will likely be new to many of the people who know me. I was also afraid that this would be seen as a cry for help or attempt to pathologize the quirkier parts of who I am rather than what it is: an honest interrogation and accounting of a set of experiences that shaped me. I was so worried about being too much for other people that I began to hide parts of myself from the world. That's no way to live. The world desperately needs far more honesty and vulnerability than we've got right now. That takes some bravery, and I'm learning to be brave for real this time.

While I'm still not totally fine, accepting that I'm not totally fine has brought me a lot closer to totally fine than I was even just a year or two ago. I still have my bad days and weeks and months, and I've also managed to build a rich life with good friendships, a stable career, a good home, a healthier body, and a healthier mind. I will always be unconventional. I'd rather live a radically honest, unconventional life than engage in the kind of hiding that I did for so long.

Actively and properly managing borderline requires an acceptance that all emotions, impulses, and desires, even the homely ones, exist. It requires me to put aside the snap judgments I make about my everyday intensity. Nothing is stupid, embarrassing, or ludicrous; it just is. Denying this is like pretending your stove isn't on fire until the entire kitchen is ablaze. Documenting my own condition in this way has been a healing thing. It's also given me insight into what parts of myself to attend to next.

The winter I began working on this collection marked a significant turning point in the way I decided to manage my condition in that I decided to manage it for real this time. It made sense, then, to begin to put together the story I had always been trying to tell as I began to tell the true story to myself. I live with a complex mental health condition, one

186

that makes the activities of daily life more difficult than they would otherwise be. In that way, it's no different than any sort of chronic health condition. Once I achieved that level of self-acceptance, the rest began to fall into place.

Gradual changes made a big difference. I can identify the impact of my condition on my thoughts and behaviors better now than ever before. I've gotten better at stepping away from situations that require a little room to think and regulate. I've found that taking my time with my thoughts, and being more intentional generally, has helped with my innate tendency to act on impulse. I'll take longer pauses to collect my thoughts. I'm usually careful about how and when I use any kind of substances. If I plan to have a serious conversation with someone, I write down what I'll say ahead of time and rehearse it.

Slowing down and feeling my own feelings have changed my life for the better. I've consciously trained my brain to use what I call "both/and" thinking. Borderline or not, no one likes a "but"; "I like you, but..."; "you did well, but..." Replacing that *but* with *and* speaks to the dialectical truth that two things can and often are true at once.

I was able to get to a place of more consistent stability with a lot of therapy, support from the people who love me, and raw, hard work. As noted in this text, dialectical behavioral therapy (DBT) is the only treatment method for borderline that has been proven through research to alleviate symptoms of the condition. It's very dull work. For someone who loves to intellectualize everything, the idea that a set of well-defined and simple skills would change things was unthinkable when I first started to practice them. In short, it felt like it was all beneath me – that I was simply too smart to struggle in the way that I did. Hitting rock bottom again and again forced my hand. As I got more comfortable with these skills, I felt silly for putting it off for so long. It was a humbling experience.

Accepting that there was anything "wrong" with me at all was a heavy task. Admitting powerlessness is the first step in recovery for a reason. It's also the hardest. While it was a simple thing, it wasn't an *easy* thing. There was a part of me that earnestly believed that I didn't deserve to get better. When the very thing you need to self-reflect on often poisons your ability to think honestly and clearly at the most inconvenient moments, the work of changing is made that much harder. Self-acceptance is not a cure-all, but it served as a starting point for all of the changing I've done.

Living a more consistent and regimented life has helped immensely. This is still a new practice. Building in regular things regularly – long walks, a morning and nighttime routine, time to recharge, time to work out – has been the single most impactful driver of change in my life over the past few years. A big part of "getting better" was accepting that I deserved to and treating myself like I deserved to.

I've had to show myself an exceptional amount of compassion while also holding myself accountable, and that's made all the difference. I've found that a lot of people are really bad at that. *I* was really bad at that. The reality is that my behavior was damaging, and it came from a place of deep sickness and persistent carelessness. Sometimes, negligence looks an awful lot like malice.

I don't always recognize the person who wrote these poems. Many of them feel alien to me, and detail experiences and emotions that seem worlds away now. I had to physically resist the impulse to forever edit the older ones, which were written in styles that I don't like, or use a limited vocabulary that I've outgrown, or worst of all, feel a little cringey. I forced myself away from my laptop many times to keep from re-writing my history. I finally finished the final draft days before release.

Human experience is heady and expansive, and is rough for all of us. I think of this as I watch the many people stroll by. Some of their heads are buried in their cellphones. Some are window-shopping. All are trying to figure it out, and I get the sense that they're all pretending a little, too. It's a very human thing to try and hide our messier parts from each other. Part of this is healthy; the liminal space between vulnerability and exhibition is a thin lace curtain. A larger part of it, however, is simple hiding.

Cleaning up my messier parts has been an adventure. I've had more love, help, and support than one man could ever earn on his own. I'm grateful for the many people who have come and gone through my life, especially for the people who came and stayed even when it was beyond difficult. The thing I was looking for was always inside of me, but I couldn't have even begun digging it out without the help of some special people. After two previous publications, I've learned that you can never thank everyone, because you'll forget someone, and then you both will feel *very* bad about it. Regardless, I will try. Love is always worth it.

My mom has been the most supportive mother a person could ask for. I know so many of us would like to believe we have the best mom ever, and I am totally convinced that I actually do. They say you shouldn't meet your heroes, but mine's been around the whole time. Thank you for being my first reader, for sitting with me in hospital rooms, hotels, parking lots, for always taking those two in the morning phone calls, for giving me room to be myself and loving me so endlessly and deeply.

I know how lucky of a thing it is to grow up with two

parents who love you. **Dad,** I love you. Your dedication to being better than your past laid the groundwork for me to be better than mine. Thank you for providing me with the foundation for all of the things that I've made of my life. I developed my love of reading (and as a result, writing) because of your bedtime stories. Pain and trauma are generational things, and I'm glad we're rattling our chains.

My late grandmother, who lives on in so much of what I do, was the single greatest influence in my early life. She, too, was a little mercurial and strange of spirit, but none of this happens without her. She was a very special woman, full of joy and whimsy and an undying love for other people – especially her family – that will long outlive her. The patch of dirt that covers her grave is the only part of the whole cemetery that is caked in wildflowers.

Thank you to **Vavo,** my father's mother, for all of her love and support. She will no doubt be a little upset about the vulgarity, but I've heard the way she talks at the television set when the Sox give up a run or Jaylen Brown turns over the ball. She's so cool, too; how many ninety-two-year-olds do you know who go gambling with their girlfriends on Fridays? Thank you for looking out for me.

Thank you to my **Aunt Terri** and **Uncle Mike,** who took me in to live with them when everything really fell apart in 2019. I owe my Aunt Terri, especially, for taking care of me for years in many ways. You've been my rock since I first moved to the city those many years ago. It won't be the same city without you in it.

I've been blessed with a wonderful, supportive extended family. **Uncle Brad** and **Aunt Erin** created a second home for me in the West. San Francisco is my sanctuary, clean of my past and where I go when I need to find my thoughts. I am so grateful for the time I've spent with you these last few years. Love you always.

Many thanks to my **Uncle Dave** and **Aunt Mary** for the very appropriate amount of beer, even though Aunt Mary is a Warriors fan. We have so much fun. Christmases spent together remain some of my favorite memories, and I appreciate deeply all that you've done for me.

My cousins Maddie, Alec, Abby, Laura, Ben, and *particularly* **David Nicholas Paul** and **his wife Kim**, who planted the seeds of subversive, radical compassion in my brain; **my cousin Rubie in New York** and **her husband Greg,** and **Aunt Del in Chicago** – without all of you, I wouldn't have had a shot.

I'm an only child, so my friends have always been my extended family. I can't start anywhere else but with **Kai.** I will never be a good enough writer to put into words the way in which I so totally and truly love you and recognize the ways in which you helped me when nothing and no one else could. I don't know what I did to deserve someone so endlessly compassionate, supportive, and thoughtful in my life, but I'd like to think I did something right given the remarkable consistency of your showing up.

Lucas, I love you. There's something very special about facing fear and uncertainty with humor and level-headedness. You've had it put together since we were fourteen. I admire your ability to keep it together under pressure. I want to be like you when I grow up. Maybe I will eventually get good at golf, and you will get good at cooking burgers after a few IPAs.

I owe many thanks to **Matt**, my "WebMD Mate" (male medical student who has seen and/or heard *way* too much about my body parts). You are genuinely one of the funniest and wisest people I've ever met. Thank you for being you. The funny thing about adult friendships is that you see someone, you have a sacred night, you put it down, and return to it over the years. Keep pushing.

Megan, thank you for being you, and being so truly kind to me from the moment we met, and showing Kai what he's really worth. You're one of the most thoughtful people I've ever had the pleasure of knowing. I wouldn't want anyone else to be stuck with me by virtue of loving Kai. You are a part of my chosen family.

Speaking of, **Schotty 'Steel Nuts' & Grit & Svenja** are their own thing entirely. There are so many times they've made me feel like the third child, a part of something. The lightweight joy of the many sleepovers I had on Gibbs were a safe space for me in a time of extreme chaos.

I met **Justin** on the very first day of college, and what more can I say except that I love him to the moon and back? We've experienced so much together so deeply. Thank you for always accepting me as I am, and for holding me when all I needed was to be held.

And then **Jess**, my Jess. There are few people who are as comfortable taking up space in a room, and being around that for all of these years has given me confidence to take up my space. I hope that I may one day have the sincerity in my work that you have in yours. Thank you for allowing me to be my whole self, unapologetically, over and over. I hope you find your peace and that its center holds.

Gabby, I love you dearly. We were all standing outside the Museum of Fine Arts at this pre-orientation thing. I was wearing this horrible pink shirt and dad shoes. You walked up to me, and having never said a word to me in my life, asked me, "Why are you wearing a pink shirt?" You've always caught me when I've fallen, and provided so much support, even from a distance.

Thanks to **Brooklyn,** my darling. You and I have been friends for many years now, and we, too, have the kind of friendship that you can return to over and over again. I am so proud of how far you've come. Thank you for always letting me rest my proverbial head on your shoulder. Keep being your badass self. I'm glad you're back.

Thank you, **Ryan,** for giving it your best, even when it was difficult and *my* best was not enough. You have this depth of spirit that isn't apparent to those who have briefly met you, but I'm so proud of you for letting that depth consume you a little bit. You're an intensely loyal and committed person, and have inspired me to make so many of the sorely needed changes to my life. Love you always.

The best thing he ever did for me was introducing me to **Mai Linh** all those years ago when they first started dating. Mai, you've been such a supportive friend and are also perfectly skilled in telling me when I'm too far in my own head, or when my head is too far up my own ass. I love our Mondays.

Even after all these years, this is also for **Sarah** – there is a lot of physical space between us. Despite it, I'm always feeling your love and support. We were in the trenches of it, and that dirty work builds bonds between people that last a while. Thank you for being my faraway friend.

I owe a thanks to **Miguel,** who it feels like has been here in my heart much longer than he actually has. I'm always seeking a gentle chaos, and I feel as though your way of being aligns nicely with this. I'm grateful to have met you.

Over the past few years, I've been trying to reconnect with my childhood, and no one has helped me do that in the same way that **Lauren (and John), Kat, Joan,** and **Don** have. Thank you for always seeing the best in me, the most lighthearted version of myself, even when I myself couldn't see it. Here's to many more decades of friendship.

I wrote about place a lot in this title, and so I'd like to thank **Roommate Greg** for helping make our good home a place to be myself, and forcing me (through example and invitation) to do things again. All good stuff, always.

My many, many **therapists and healthcare providers** from over the years have given me the space to understand and accept myself in a way I never thought I could. **Dr. Gold** and **Jim** were instrumental in helping me make it out of my youth in one piece. **Dr. K** – thank you, thank you. You've helped me access a part of myself that I didn't know existed. I've never had someone so committed to my getting better, and it's made all the difference.

A special thanks to my **crackpot coworkers – especially Ross, Parker, Brandon, Chase,** and **Sarah** – even if they didn't know why I was a little out there, they were always okay with me being out there. **Heather** – I'm so proud to call you my friend. Thank you for making the motions of day-to-day corporate life so much more fun for so long.

Finally, I owe a deep debt to the various individuals I met briefly along my road to recovery. I met these people in various states of distress, theirs and mine. I haven't spoken with any of them in years, and wouldn't know where to find them if I tried, but I think of them often. Thank you, **Kyle, Cassandra, Chad, Rihanna, Chris, Louisa, Eli, Kat, Ken, Sonia, Ollie, Heidi, Wilson, Jen, Lianna,** and **every other hurting person out there** who ever felt consumed by it. This book is for you as much as it is for me.

Resources

THERE ARE MORE PEOPLE THAN EVER who are living with various mental health conditions and disorders. These are not fun times for anyone, with all the disorder, hate, chaos, and needless violence. We're subjected to it constantly, and we were never meant to be.

These resources, accurate as of the time this book went to print (early November 2025), are meant to serve as a starting point for those who are looking for help but don't know where to begin.

While **988** remains the most widely known hotline for people experiencing crisis, recent events – including the defunding of specialized support services for queer people – have made it a controversial resource. Alternatives do exist. The **National Alliance on Mental Illness** (https://nami.org/help) maintains a confidential hotline, 1-800-950-NAMI (6264). You can also text "HelpLine" to 62640 or e-mail helpline@nami.org. Services are available from 10 a.m. to 10 p.m. ET, Monday through Friday.

Queer people in need of support have multiple options. The **Trevor Project** (https://www.thetrevorproject.org/) maintains a similar hotline specifically meant to support young queer and trans people. They can be reached at 866-4-U-TREVOR (866-488-7386) 24 hours a day, seven days a week. The **Trans Lifeline** (https://translifeline.org) offers specialized support for trans people. They can be reached at 877-565-8860.

Historically marginalized groups have unique needs that are best understood by people who share their lived experiences. The **BlackLine** (www.callblackline.com) is designed to provide support and resources to Black,

Brown, and Indigenous members of the queer community. They can be reached at 1 (800) 604-5841.

Expectant and new mothers in need of support can contact the **National Maternal Mental Health Hotline,** which is staffed 24/7, by calling or texting 1-833-TLC-MAMA (833-852-6262).

Veterans who are struggling with their mental health can get help by reaching out to the **Veterans Crisis Line** (www.veteranscrisisline.net), either by dialing 988 and pressing 1, or texting 838255. You do not need to be enrolled in VA benefits or healthcare to call.

Hotlines alone will not bring about societal change. A holistic approach with the people closest to the pain leading the conversation is the best way to ensure everyone's needs are met. I'm one person with one experience, and I can't speak to the needs of all other people. My experiences have taught me, however, that there are many contributing factors to mental health issues – violence, poverty, discrimination, et cetera. All of these must be addressed as part of any lasting solution.

I was so very lucky to have access to the best mental healthcare in the world, and getting healthy was *still* a struggle. I cannot begin to comprehend how much more difficult being poor or non-white or a non-native English speaker makes it. Until we fundamentally alter the way we approach mental health issues and addiction, little will change. Right now, it's very easy to become disillusioned with the prospect of change in any facet of public life. Every single fascistic government in recent history has at some point set its sights on people experiencing mental illness, and they will do it again. The soft violence of this system is meant to break spirits long before it breaks bones. Don't let it.